COLOURS OF ARCHITECTURE

COLOURS OF ARCHITECTURE

COLOURED GLASS IN CONTEMPORARY BUILDINGS

ANDREW MOOR

MITCHELL BEAZLEY

COLOURS OF ARCHITECTURE
by ANDREW MOOR

This book is dedicated to my wife Patrice, who encouraged me
to embark on a third book, and my children Edward, Osbert, and
Mariette, who make it worthwhile.

First published in Great Britain in 2006 by Mitchell Beazley,
an imprint of Octopus Publishing Group Limited,
2–4 Heron Quays, London E14 4JP.

A CIP catalogue record for this book is available
from the British Library.

ISBN-13: 978 1 84533 123 8
ISBN-10: 1 84533 123 0

The author and publishers will be grateful for any information which
will assist them in keeping future editions up to date. Although all
reasonable care has been taken in the preparation of this book,
neither the publishers nor the author can accept any liability for
any consequences arising from the use thereof, or the information
contained therein.

Commissioning editor Hannah Barnes-Murphy
Executive art editor Sarah Rock
Senior editor Emily Anderson
Editor Kirsty Seymour-Ure
Design John Round Design
Indexer Helen Snaith
Production Gary Hayes
Architectural research Hattie Hartmann

Printed and bound in China by Toppan Printing Company Ltd

PAGE 1 **BIG POPPY**, San José, California, 2003:
by Nick Lyle and Jean Whitesavage. This detail shows the
enamelled and mouth-blown glass elements. The project
includes 12 glass skylights for six light-rail stations,
commissioned by the Santa Clara Valley Transit Authority.

PAGE 2 **"RAIGS X"** (X-ray), Barcelona, Spain, 1997, by:
José Castrillo. Detail from panel made for doctor's clinic.

RIGHT **MUSAC**, Leon, Spain, 2005, by: Mansilla & Tunon.
A new cultural centre by these two ground-breaking
architectural theorists, who are now winning competitions
and creating striking new architecture.

CONTENTS

Colours of Architecture is about the transformation in architectural glass art that has taken place over the past 20 years. A technique, almost unchanged for a thousand years, has been revolutionized.

When I sat down to write this book, I remembered an incident that happened when I was writing my first book, *Contemporary Stained Glass.* I was giving a lecture to some architectural students. A young woman asked, "How come you're involved in an art form that's been going downhill for 700 years?" I was struck by the truth behind this question. Stained glass reached a pinnacle in the 13th century, and never again matched it.

I believe now, in its new forms of expression, it could start to rival those iconic and legendarily magical creations.

Two people have been pivotal in helping to make this book a reality. The architectural journalist Hattie Hartmann helped me with the research and text. My brother Richard organized the pictures, dealt with the photographers, and helped me with a huge amount of organization. For my wife and children, the past six months have meant my disappearing into the basement at every spare moment "to work on the book". It is good to be back.

I hope this book illuminates the exciting world of colour, glass, and architecture, and suggests and fertilizes ideas in many areas of what can be done with this extraordinary medium – glass.

Andrew Moor

LEFT **SALVATION ARMY INTERNATIONAL CHAPEL**, London, England, 2004. Architect: Carpenter Lowings Architects. Suspended in a contemporary building is a burning orange chapel – the glowing heart of the Salvation Army world headquarters. The glass is laminated and coloured with an etched exterior.

THE BACKGROUND

By 1990 architectural glass art had been in a state of denial and dysfunction for many years. The central technique used by almost all architectural glass artists had remained unchanged for more than a thousand years. Throughout the 20th century, artists had developed a new language in terms of design, but the basic method used to execute these designs was still essentially a medieval technology.

This has now changed. In the space of little more than a decade or so, "leaded glass" has finally been supplanted as the major method of putting glass, art, and architecture together. So, how and why has this come about?

Largely it is a reflection of how modern architects and builders think about buildings. Today, the modules, the contexts, and the fundamental aesthetic language that we aspire to have all changed. Leaded glass evolved at a time when glass could only be made in small panels of 60–90cm (24–36in). This is the ideal width of a stained glass window. Panels of this width can be stacked up on top of each other and, with a little additional support to stop them sagging, can become a tall thin window. Stained glass is supple, flexible, and durable, but it has no structural strength, no intrinsic rigidity, and requires structure to keep it erect.

This is not what architects want. Architects want entire walls of glass, not slitlike apertures in solid walls. They want a seamless, frameless, weightless experience. They want glass panels more than a metre wide and at least 2.5m (8ft) tall. This they can effortlessly incorporate into their buildings, without any added structure. Leaded glass has no place in this aesthetic ideal. It speaks a beautiful language, but it is not the language of modern architecture.

ABOVE **BIRMINGHAM INTERNATIONAL CONVENTION CENTRE**, Birmingham, England, 1991: by Alexander Beleschenko. Many thin strips of printed and mouth-blown glass are sandwiched between two layers of float glass, creating this 30sqm (320sqft) suspended glass artwork.

ABOVE **BIRMINGHAM INTERNATIONAL CONVENTION CENTRE** Despite the artwork weighing nearly 1000 kg (2200 lb), the delicate detailing and engineering give the impression of something floating in mid-air. The design is a perfect combination of the solid and predictable with the exquisite and asymmetric.

HEART TENT, DIPLOMATIC CLUB, Riyadh, Saudi Arabia, 1989: by Frei Otto. Often dubbed the Buckminster Fuller of Europe, German architect Frei Otto spent a lifetime pushing the boundaries with his tensile structures. This landmark structure, cable-tensioned and tentlike, grappled with every possible glass challenge and technical frontier.

HEART TENT, DIPLOMATIC CLUB The painting, carried out by a team of five craftspeople led by Bettina Otto (Frei's daughter), took more than a year to complete. The work includes both transparent and opaque enamels and was the first work of this scale ever undertaken using toughened float glass.

Thus for most of the 1900s, despite the patronage in the early days of the century of Frank Lloyd Wright, Charles Rennie Mackintosh, and the influential Bauhaus movement of the 1920s, stained glass never really found support from modern architects. It remained parked in a backwater, a prisoner of its own much-loved but completely outdated technology.

This state of affairs was virtually unchanged until the 1990s. But little more than a decade later, architectural glass art is becoming a partner to architecture and, often, a language for architects to explore – expanding the vocabulary of materials, colours, and form. We now see an industry that has totally reinvented itself. It is a transformation

that few inside the world of glass fully perceive because it has seemed so inevitable and so logical.

Today there are few "stained-glass artists": they are now glass artists, or architectural glass artists, or perhaps just artists who work in glass. Fewer projects in contemporary buildings are in leaded glass. The language of design and techniques has evolved, and the potential for the medium to be incorporated into new buildings has expanded hugely.

NEW TECHNIQUES

It is possible to define these gradual evolutions by noting a few individual events that have acted as symbolic markers, reflecting the changing spirit of the times.

Alexander Beleschenko's Stockley Park window of 1986 (*see Contemporary Stained Glass* by Andrew Moor) was one of his first major projects, and revealed his commitment to working without the confines of lead. His "sandwich" technique involved cutting mouth-blown glass – used for centuries in leaded glass – and sandwiching the pieces together between two layers of toughened glass. The result, seen in the panels shown on page 8 from the Birmingham Convention Centre, can be beautiful and delicate. The technique's disadvantage is the tendency of the glass to act as a mirror, obscuring the coloured glass behind, and the huge weight of the triple-layered panels. Yet the outstanding feature of Beleschenko's scheme in

ABOVE **TATE GALLERY, ST IVES**, England, 1994, 4.85 x 4.95m (15.9 x 16.2ft): by the artist Patrick Heron. This window was installed as two glass panels with a reinforcing glass fin 32mm (1.3in) thick. It was one of the first large-scale projects using antique glass laminated to float glass.

ABOVE RIGHT **THE MERSEYWAY**, Stockport, England, 1995: by Graham Jones. This detail from a large scheme by the artist shows how laminated antique glass windows can create the most painterly effects, using all the techniques of stained glass without the graphic lead line.

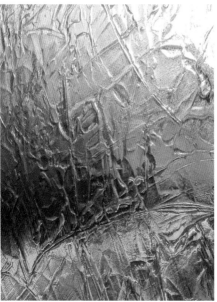

TOP LEFT **INTERNAL WALL, HOTEL AUBIER**,
Neuchatel, Switzerland, 1991, 5.4 x 5.6m (17.7 x 18.4ft):
designed and made by Udo Zembok. The work was made
entirely with painted enamels fired onto float glass and
laminated to toughened glass.

TOP RIGHT **CHELSEA FLOWER SHOW**, London, 2004:
by Fusion Glass. This panel shows a typical slumped glass
texture. The glass, which has no repeated pattern, appears
formed almost organically into this richly textured surface.

ABOVE **ING BANK HQ**, Amsterdam, The Netherlands,
1987, 150sqm (1,600sqft). This project was made by
laminating antique glass to toughened float glass, leaving
clear areas to contrast with the textures of the antique
glass and the void of float glass.

Birmingham is how successfully he made the glass appear to be weightless and to float in the air. This technique has not been widely used, perhaps because laminating (or bonding) antique (mouth-blown) glass directly to the base glass achieves many of the same objectives.

Laminated antique glass

Laminating antique glass to float glass is widespread now. The great advantage of this method is that large panels can be made (*see* St Ives Tate Gallery, UK, 1994 on p.10) that are structurally strong, but retain all the magical quality of real mouth-blown glass without the surrounding lead. For those who are trained in stained glass this is a satisfying evolution because all the beauty of colour and texture and the technique of stained glass are still available. Only the lead is missing.

Enamels on float glass

Enamels on glass are much more widely used now than they were 20 years ago.

The enamels themselves are not different, and have been in use for many years. A more significant change perhaps is the lower cost of kilns to handle large sheets of glass; these also take up less room than they used to and are easier to operate via a computer program.

Enamels can be brushed or rubbed onto glass, they can be screen-printed, or they can be airbrushed. Amazing results can be achieved but, as with all techniques, experience is needed to master them, and continual experimentation necessary to reap their potential. Many artists were, and some still are, suspicious of the capacity of float glass to achieve any significant result, in the same way that some painters will not work with acrylics because the quality of textures and colours cannot match oil paint.

Sandblasted glass

The sandblasting of glass to achieve gradations of transparency and translucency and to create relief shapes

ABOVE **DETAIL OF DOT MATRIX**, Al Faisaliah Centre, Riyadh, Saudi Arabia, 2002: by Brian Clarke. This detail, taken from a fish image, shows how, by working with larger-scale dots on two surfaces of glass, Clarke finds an ambiguity of image and abstraction.

RIGHT **CHURCH OF THE HOLY SPIRIT**, Friedberg, Germany, 2004. This is one window in a large church project. All the blue background has been screen-printed onto float glass; the yellow and green fragments have been bonded on afterward.

in the glass has been around for more than 100 years. Some artists like to add colour to the abraded surface. There are many different products individual artists and craftspeople use to achieve their results and the effects can be fabulous. They often have a brilliance of colour, coupled with strong texture, that is not easily matched by other methods.

Slumped glass

Twenty years ago this was an almost unheard of medium. A few individuals, such as Florian Lechner, were making extraordinary slumped-glass features, but mostly it was unknown. Even in 1990 it was still hard to get a piece of slumped glass to go through a toughening plant, but now slumped glass is marketed all over the world. It has a texture that is organic – smooth like glass, but also rough in a strange, natural way. It shimmers in light and each piece is unique. In recent years, those with large kilns have learned how to fuse many layers of glass together, creating great thick slabs of glass. Fused glass is a costly product because the long cooling period ties up expensive equipment for days, or even weeks, but

the decreasing cost of the kilns, and the magical appearance of 100mm (4in) thick slabs of glass, make the product tempting despite the cost.

Pigmented lamination

This industrial process has been carried out by hand for some time, but has now been developed by a global corporation. Vanceva Glass is now all over the world, and illustrated here quite extensively.

Film on glass

In the 21st century the glass business has been invaded by the magic of plastic, by the computer, and all the marvels arising from a combination of the two. Coloured films are available that can be stuck onto float glass and are remarkably durable. The range of colours available is extensive, and by mixing different layers and adding in etched film the variety of what can be achieved is enormous.

Then there is digitally printed film, which can be stuck onto glass or even laminated between two layers of glass. This can have all the advantages of four-colour printing, including the relatively low cost, the universal language of the

design and execution process, and the impermanence for those who like to organize a new look every few years.

IS THIS ART?

At least one artist expressed concern about my plan to mix the designs in glass of artists and architects in this book, and said, "There is a distinction between the sort of decorative devices that architects may do and art". However, this book is attempting to show what can be done with glass, whether as art or as an ally for the architect in his or her wish to design beautiful and functional buildings.

None the less, the viewpoint raises important issues. We have not yet begun to understand all the ways in which glass can be used to add detail or decoration to buildings. Hopefully, one of the things this book will illustrate is how much can be achieved, and how simply, and at what relatively low cost in relation to impact, by "doing" things to the glass.

Is there something wrong with using glass as a decorative device? Is "Art" to be distinguished from "art"? The underlying truth is that a complex continuum joins art and decoration. Anyone seeing Frank

ABOVE This shows some of the facilities (in approximately 1992) at the Franz Mayer Studios in Munich, Germany, one of the large studios that assist artists in manufacturing their work using modern technology and manufacturing equipment.

ABOVE RIGHT This picture shows part of Ken Leap's Bayonne Station project (*see* p.77) being manufactured at the Derix Glass Studios near Wiesbaden, Germany. A craftsman is airbrushing enamels onto the glass prior to firing.

ABOVE **ST ANDREAS**, Essen, Germany, 1993: by Jochem
Poensgen. By means of the sandwich technique, and using
simple industrial glass in layers to create shimmering
patterns, Poensgen demonstrates the art of "decoration"
by the architectural glass artist.

Gehry's Guggenheim Museum in Bilbao, Spain, must surely feel they are standing in front of a fantastic, monumental work of art; indeed, the exhibitions inside may often fail to live up to the building itself. Art, architecture, and design are bedfellows that tumble around together, impinging on and influencing each other – sometimes competing for the same space.

ARCHITECTS AND ARTISTS

Whether these two "professions" are brother and sister or merely distant cousins is debatable. There have always been artist/architects (the Gaudís, the Lloyd Wrights, and the Gehrys) who truly span the divide with their originality, their drawing skills, and their capacity to change the visual language. But the languages of architecture and art are in many ways different languages, with quite different objectives, although there are moments or contexts when they merge.

Perhaps the greatest architectural glass artist of the last century is the German glass designer Jochem Poensgen. In his inspiring pamphlet *Glaskunst in Architektur* (1987) he urges glass artists to strive for "civil inattention": that is, for their work to be experienced but not noticed. "The perfect work of architectural art will not cry out for attention but will meet a casual reception." One powerful feature of his work is the element of repetition. In his 1993 church windows in Essen he sets up a pattern in the glass and repeats it without deviation, without feeling that, as an artist, he has to be disturbing or interrupting a rhythm. Much of architecture is about creating rhythms. The nature of architectural detailing is often to establish a repeated motif that in its repetition achieves substance. One pediment might be boring; a series can be strong. One column might achieve little; a line of columns establishes rhythms. Poensgen's work may serve as a model for how architectural glass artists can work with architects to develop devices that enhance buildings, but do not necessarily aspire to be art. Perhaps, as so often in life, it is when we give up trying that we achieve our goal. Sometimes it can be the very modesty of the original intent that is the key to ultimate success.

CONTEXTS

The wealth of contexts in which enamelled and laminated glass can be used to successful effect is enormous. Instead of a simple dot matrix to reduce solar gain, images – photographs, drawings, graphics – can be explored. The flat plane of a building can be turned into sinuous curves by the use of graduated tones. Skyscrapers of the future may be highlighted with bands of coloured glass, reflecting and transmitting light.

Some places are more obvious choices than others – stairwells that have external glazing offer an ideal location, where it is possible to create a continuous tall "painting", visible from the exterior. The interior, by contrast, offers a temporary stimulation to a person moving from one floor to another. Stairwells are not inhabited space: they are transient space. As glass is a very potent medium, transient space is often the most appropriate to design

for because the experience may be momentary and the drama may be entirely suitable, whereas inhabited space may need something more passive.

It seems too obvious to state, but almost anywhere that glass is being used can provide a context for decorating the glass. It is the architects of vision who are taking up this opportunity, and those who enjoy collaborating with artists who are best able to achieve their goals.

TOP **ILLUSTRATION BY STUART REID**, 2003. This apparently fantastical illustration is an element of a well-researched proposal that Stuart Reid published as part of a manifesto for the development of an area of Toronto, Canada.

ABOVE **"CELESTIAL PASSAGE"**, Baltimore/Washington International Airport, Maryland, USA, 2005. Antique glass laminated to float. In the Southwest Airlines terminal this window will be seen by embarking and disembarking passengers, acting as a night beacon for those arriving at the airport.

ARCHITECTURE

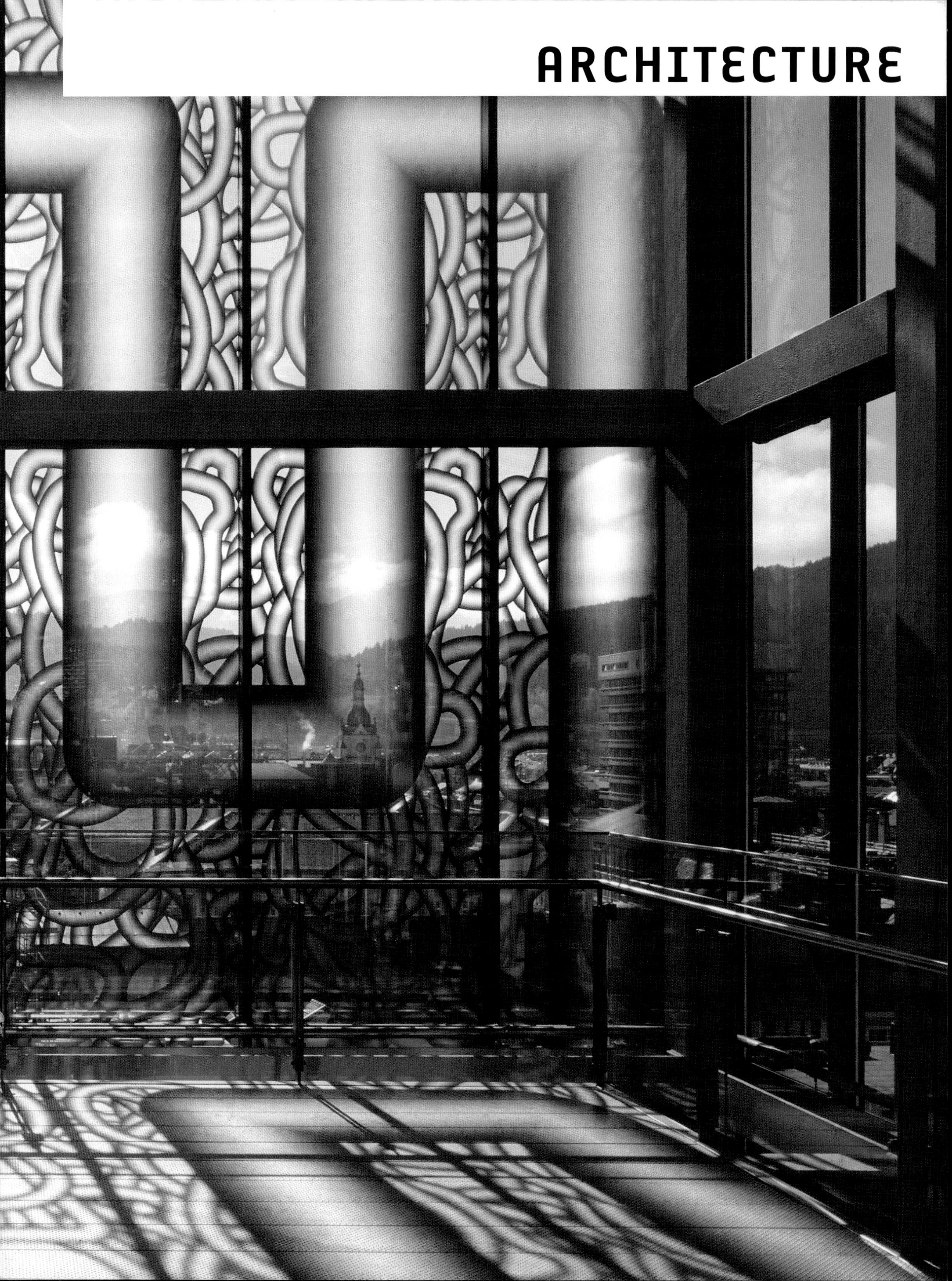

Glass forms a major part of the external skin and interior dividing walls of contemporary buildings. Is is also used for balustrades, elevators, desks, and almost anything else that can be thought of.

It is not difficult to add colour to glass, as well as patterns, textures, gradations of tones, and other qualities, all of which add to the enormous versatility of the medium. This is a language that is available at a reasonable cost, and that can transform the character of a building – yet one that, surprisingly, is not widely exploited.

Glass and colour are a powerful combination. As seen in many of the images in this book, the use of colour as part of a building's exterior has a powerful impact on the immediate surroundings. And when the glass is experienced from the interior the internal space can be transformed.

It is quite rare to see glass art that is simply a part of the "decoration" of a building, and many artists would be offended to hear their work described as ornamental. But it is noticeable that many of the features included in this Architecture section were achieved in collaboration with an artist. For example, the collaboration between the artist Liam Gillick and the Terry Farrell Partnership, shown on pp.54–5, shows how successful modest intervention can be. The work has a high impact level, though its content is minimal; it had a relatively low cost; and, perhaps owing to its modesty and simplicity of concept, is well integrated into the building.

The idea lurks in the philosophy of some architects that art is added only to buildings that have "failed" and need to distract the eye. This is a sad view, perhaps belonging to those architects who regard the arrival of human occupants as a death blow to their aesthetic creation. To some extent the problem lies in the relationship between artist and architect. One tends to have a view of the particular, the other of the whole; one likes to make statements, the other is trying to synthesize a myriad interests. But when they work together successfully, the results can be brilliant.

PREVIOUS PAGE **TOWN HALL**, Innsbruck, Austria, 2002. Architect: Dominique Perrault. Artist: Peter Kogler. The image shows one part of this five-floor masterpiece of art and architecture. Printed in black, four original designs are interwoven, like a Max Escher illustration, to create a complex, three-dimensional narrative.

ABOVE **NOVARTIS CAMPUS**, Basle, Switzerland, 2005. Architect: Diener & Diener. Artist: Helmut Federle with architect Gerikd Wiederin. Coloured glass panels, arranged on three different planes and supported on vertical bars, create a shifting pattern of colour across this large façade.

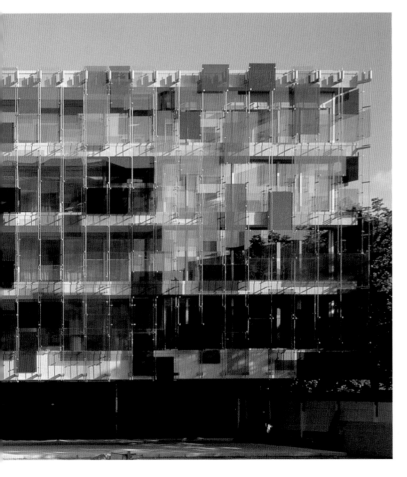

TOP RIGHT, MIDDLE RIGHT, & BOTTOM RIGHT
EURALILLE, Lille, France, 1995. Architect: Jean Nouvel.
This link between two large buildings forms part of a huge,
commercial, multiple-use project in Lille. The exterior picture
shows the mixture of coloured and black-and-white digital
films used. From one of the office areas inside we see how the
imagery has been used to obscure the exterior view, which is
largely highways and cars. It is typical of such an adventurous
architect as Nouvel that he would utilize, at the same time, a
state-of-the-art technology.

Among the architectural community enamelled glass is often known as fritted glass. The word "frit" comes from a Latin word meaning "roast" or "fry". Fritted glass is glass that has had an enamel image or pattern fired or baked into its surface. Firing is done by slow heating and slow cooling, but often the process will take place while the glass is being toughened. In toughening, the glass is rapidly heated and rapidly cooled, thereby trapping fast-moving molecules inside a skin of slower-moving molecules. This gives greatly increased strength and flexibility to the material, and also means that should it break the glass will fragment into thousands of tiny pieces rather than large, dangerously sharp shards. This is structural glass as we see it used in the construction of buildings all over the world.

All toughened glass can easily have images of any sort printed onto its surface. However, to print one image on one piece of glass is a lengthy process. A screen must be made from an original full-size image, then this must be set up in the press, the positioning exactly checked, and the piece of glass printed. But the printing of further pieces of glass is relatively

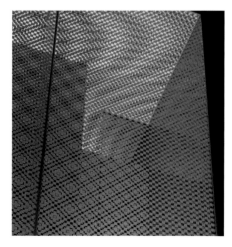

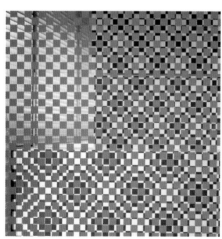

ABOVE, ABOVE RIGHT, & FAR RIGHT **LOUIS VUITTON STORE**, Nagoya, Japan, 1999. Architect: Jun Aoki. Japanese architect Aoki has made a speciality of transforming glass into a semi-transparent membrane, with an appearance not unlike Japanese paper screens.

This, his first Louis Vuitton store, in Nagoya, demonstrates Aoki's use of patterns – in this case printed on both sides of the glass to create shimmering moiré effects that are at once formal and restrained, but which attract the eye and create a memorable feature.

OFFICE AND RESIDENTIAL BUILDING, Vienna, Austria, 2003. Architect: Delugan Meissl. This five-storey office and residential building has 105 screen-printed glass panels. There are two horizontal images and one vertical image, yet the whole somehow avoids appearing endlessly repetitive. At night the interior light is trapped by the screen, and from the exterior modesty screening is achieved. In sunlight the panels cast magical shadows on the balcony floors.

fast – thus the use of repeated images is a way of greatly reducing costs, though this steep curve starts to flatten off after about ten panels.

The opportunities this process offers to architects are enormous –solar gain can be hugely reduced by enamelled images on glass. Fritting does not have to be white dots, or white squares, any more than manifestations to prevent people bumping into glass have to be dots or squares. Almost anything is possible, and a whole new language is available in terms of the form and visible texture of buildings' façades.

1 HOSPITAL PHARMACY INSTITUTE, Basle, Switzerland, 1998. This photograph, taken through a window into the internal atrium, shows how the image of dots is created on the glass.

2 HOSPITAL PHARMACY INSTITUTE The simple block building is given character and identity through the powerful features of colour and a graphic pattern. The pattern emphasizes the way lines converge in perspective.

Herzog and de Meuron are pioneers of new approaches to building façades. Whether opaque or transparent, these buildings change according to the time of day and the weather, and, like pointillist paintings, they read differently from a distance than from close range.

The Hospital Pharmacy Institute in the Rosetti grounds of Basle's Kantonsspital in Switzerland is clad entirely in square panes of glass screen-printed with grids of green dots. The glass is supported on steel struts that hold it out from an inner wall of perforated steel panels. At a distance, the building reads as a vibrant and shimmering glazed box akin to op art. The play between the two different dot patterns creates a moiré effect.

In their project in Mulhouse, France, for Swiss company Ricola (*see* pp.24–5), the architects clad the warehouse in an inexpensive polycarbonate, screen-printed with a repeated leaf motif from a photograph by Karl Blossfeldt. Printed imagery became a key concept

1

again in their Eberswalde Technical School Library. The three-storey building is clad in glass and cast concrete that has been screen-printed with photographs by the artist Thomas Ruff. Each horizontal band is printed with a single repeated image. The wallpaper-like treatment, in silvery hues, has a lightness and transparency that is both elegant and engaging.

The Brandenburg Technical University library in Cottbus (*see* pp.26–7) takes the use of screen-printing in the cladding one step further, resulting in a kind of dematerialization of the façade. All the exterior glazed panels are screen-printed with enormous random letters. The resulting abstract pattern provides a degree of privacy as well as sun-screening for the interior. By day, from the inside, the screen-printed letters dissolve into a luminous white screen. By night the pattern is bold and abstract, like calligraphy gone wild.

3 **EBERSWALDE TECHNICAL SCHOOL LIBRARY**, Eberswalde, Germany, 1999. An external close-up shows how effective repeated images can be. The entrance porches offer the chance for the images to be expressed in a different way.

4 **EBERSWALDE TECHNICAL SCHOOL LIBRARY** In the connecting corridor we see how sunlight casts images onto the floor and walls, reminiscent of the way stained-glass windows can throw coloured patterns around dark Gothic interiors.

5 **EBERSWALDE TECHNICAL SCHOOL LIBRARY** From a distance the photographic images revert from the specific into merely textural ornamental forms, which create rhythmic ripples in the exterior façade.

6 **RICOLA WAREHOUSE**,
Mulhouse, France, 1993.
Such a well-publicized project
may have encouraged more
architects to follow suit, exploiting
this simple device of a repeated
image on the façade. It encloses
the space but still allows natural
light to flood into the interior.

7 8 **RICOLA
WAREHOUSE**
This single-colour print appears
like an ornamental relief
moulding, and so adds a
three-dimensional quality to
the single plane of the exterior.

9

10

11

9 COTTBUS INFORMATION, COMMUNICATIONS AND MEDIA CENTRE, Brandenburg Technical University, Cottbus, Germany, 2004. Rising like a medieval castle with its mythologically white and shining exterior, this library building slowly reveals itself to be covered in a jumble of random letters.

10 COTTBUS INFORMATION, COMMUNICATIONS AND MEDIA CENTRE The more you look, the more it appears as though every panel is different; the repeating nature of the images has been skilfully disguised, partially by the many changes in scale of the actual letters.

12

11 **COTTBUS INFORMATION, COMMUNICATIONS AND MEDIA CENTRE** The lettering is noticeable but discreet. The printing is expressed in dots that fade towards the edges, allowing clear vision through from the interior, yet significantly reducing the light levels.

12 **COTTBUS INFORMATION, COMMUNICATIONS AND MEDIA CENTRE** At night the lettering shows up against the bulkheads, emphasizing the building's undulating curves. The enamel acts as a modest filter to the interior lighting, from both inside and outside.

1 **UNIVERSITY OF UTRECHT LIBRARY**, The Netherlands, 2004. The form of the building is very stark. Moulded black concrete contrasts with a uniform glazing module, combining to create a monolithic rectangular box.

2 **UNIVERSITY OF UTRECHT LIBRARY** The printed glass panels are shown here at night, illuminated from within, providing a soft semitransparent filter between interior and exterior.

Ranked by some alongside the Swiss partnership Herzog and de Meuron, Dutch architect Wiel Arets is highly influential and becoming more widely renowned, both as a writer and theorist and as a practising creator of challenging, poetic, but austere buildings.

Arets' most recent building, the library of the University of Utrecht in The Netherlands, is, from the outside, a large dark square box – a classic modernist structure. In contrast to this austere aesthetic, the entire external surface (the glass, the concrete cladding, and the actual window glass) is covered with a repeated printed motif: a photographic image of reeds – perhaps selected because of its reference to papyrus, paper, books, and hence the library. This simple and inexpensive device, developed in collaboration with the photographer Kim Zwarts, transforms both the external and the internal experience of the library.

From the outside the screen-printed motif changes as the viewer draws nearer to the building, evolving from the merest hint of a texture, into a pattern, and finally an image. At night the glazing shimmers slightly as the light is diffused through the softening lattice of the translucent printing, as if a semitransparent curtain were enclosing the working areas.

The interior experience of the building is also transformed by this printed image – whether in direct sunlight or under cloudy skies, at dusk or at dawn, the diaphanous membrane between interior and exterior constantly changes. Sometimes the light seems to rest on the image, making it bright, distinct, and shimmery, and obscuring the outside. In a different light the outside can be seen remarkably clearly through the spaces between the images.

Arets has designed the interior of this building to be a monumental space, with tall volumes and large windows that, but for the image on the glass, would allow an excess of light into the building. This light could potentially damage the books and destroy the sense of space. However, with the light diffused by the printed image, the space is enclosed and the harsh glare softened, creating a large yet intimate interior that is a haven for concentration and study.

4

3 **UNIVERSITY OF UTRECHT LIBRARY**
Every panel of glass is printed with the same image, of papyrus reeds – an appropriate reference for a library. The concrete also has the image impressed into its surface.

4 **UNIVERSITY OF UTRECHT LIBRARY**
The scale and drama of the internal spaces, revealed here by the human figures, shows the need for reducing ambient light. The enamelled glass has allowed the architect to modulate the light.

3

Erick van Egeraat has a practice (Erick van Egeraat Associated Architects, or EEA) that specializes in mixing forms with a fluid approach to materials to create exciting buildings that have slightly unpredictable elements. The use of screen-printed glass has been an ongoing feature – creating natural stone patterns in his ING building of 1997, or using lettering to create moiré effects in The Netherlands Embassy building in Warsaw, 2004, and again in the ING Budapest building of 2004.

The InHolland University building in Rotterdam uses panels of screen-printed glass both for exterior cladding and within the interior atrium spaces. Glazed panels printed with random patterns in two different blues function both as spatial dividers that maintain a partial transparency, and as architectural motifs within the overall structure.

At the Liget Centre in Budapest, a repeated vertical pattern of letters is used to create a balustrade in the glass façade. From the exterior this not only acts as a privacy screen but also helps to define the form and shape of the building. What from a distance is no more than a texture, a ribbon of different colour or tone, achieves interesting particularity as one draws closer.

The city hall of Alphen aan den Rijn (see pp.32–3), is an example of van Egeraat's bold use of curvilinear form. From a distance the intricate patterns on the glass form a soft texture. As one approaches the building, especially at night, the shapes achieve a dramatic, explosive quality. Inside, the organic, weaving forms seem to be changing endlessly, although in fact there are only nine separate original images. The glass, with its web of natural texture, helps both to enclose and to define the space.

1

1 **LIGET CENTRE**, Budapest, Hungary, 2001. This picture shows the printed modesty screens from the exterior as seen from a distance, where the effect of rippling vertical lines is created.

2 **LIGET CENTRE** From inside, the vertical lines emerge as random letters, creating an intriguing graphic device that adds a decorative detail to the building, while also having some functional purpose.

2

3

4

3 INHOLLAND UNIVERSITY,

Rotterdam, The Netherlands, 2000. The printed glass feature, used as cladding, is more interesting than a plain block colour. It suggests ideas for stairwells that could excite interest from both inside and out.

INHOLLAND UNIVERSITY

4 This detail shows the design printed on the glass used in the internal and external glazing. In the interior the design allows some vision through the glass, while maintaining a psychological separation.

5

6

7

8

5 **CITY HALL**, Alphen aan
den Rijn, The Netherlands,
2002. This eccentrically shaped,
curvilinear building is clad in
panels of enamelled glazing,
which create a shimmering
external surface.

6 **CITY HALL** This small
detail shows how the half-
tone white dots used to make
the images create graded tonal
variations, making the overall
image natural and organic,
like smoke drifting in the wind.

7 **CITY HALL** Here the
weaving organic shapes
on the glass reveal themselves
as abstracted, two-dimensional
images of trees. We see their
thin spindly trunks wrapping
around the building's base.

8 **CITY HALL**
The effect of this cleverly
orchestrated illusion is dramatic
and, at the same time, functional
– reducing but not destroying
the transparency of the entire
external skin of the building.

Highly regarded German architects Matthias Sauerbruch and Louisa Hutton started using colour while doing small residential projects in their early days as a practice. They tend to use blocks of abstract colour, influenced by the Bauhaus artist and theorist Josef Albers. Colour is a risky approach to architectural design, as it can easily be overwhelming, but when it is successful it can result in a building with a strong and rich identity.

Sauerbruch and Hutton use colour to achieve many different aims, some practical and some more intangible – reflecting ideas about image, identity, environmental impact, and status and aspiration. Their buildings do not blend seamlessly into the surroundings; they assert themselves, yet they are subtle and enduring.

Their use of colours in the external glazing of buildings often appears much stronger from the exterior, where the colours are seen in combination with each other, than from the interior, where they are mainly experienced in isolation. Inside, shifts in colour from room to room or from floor to floor give each space a unique atmosphere.

In the amoeba-like Photonics Centre in Berlin colour was used on a large scale through the introduction of

1

PHOTONICS CENTRE, Berlin, Germany, 1998. Coloured blinds, hung within the façade's double skin, are used to dramatic effect to enliven the building's presence within an office park in a Berlin suburb.

2

horizontal Venetian blinds in 36 different shades, alluding to the theme of optical research that is carried on inside the building. Although the glazing is clear, the varying colour spectrum of the blinds behind the undulating façade is a simple solution with high visual impact.

The seven-storey 10,000sq-m (110,000sq-ft) Pharmacological Research Laboratories for Boehringer Ingelheim (*see* pp.36–7)) has an "intelligent" glazed outer skin, screen-printed with eight different colours and made up of hinged louvres that can individually track the motion of the sun. This provides extremely efficient thermal performance as well as achieving the idiosyncratic appearance that the architects wanted, expressing the singular and unpredictable quality of research.

In the Berlin Police and Fire Station (*see* pp.38–9), colours ranging from red to green symbolize the transition from danger to safety.

3

PHOTONICS CENTRE
2 From a distance the blinds read as coloured glazing, with unusual patterns of reflections that are magnified by the organic form of the building.

PHOTONICS CENTRE
3 The Venetian blinds create a delicate and irregular play of light in the interior, quite different from the effects achieved with coloured glass. The blinds can be controlled individually by the occupants.

4

5

4 **BOEHRINGER INGELHEIM PHARMACOLOGICAL RESEARCH LABORATORIES**, Biberach, Germany, 2002. An outer skin of colourful glass louvres, centrally controlled by a building management system, provides solar shading and creates a striking image.

5 **BOEHRINGER INGELHEIM PHARMACOLOGICAL RESEARCH LABORATORIES** From the office interiors the impact of the colour on the glass louvres, which consist of single panes of toughened glass with screen-printed enamel, is far less visible.

6 **BOEHRINGER INGELHEIM PHARMACOLOGICAL RESEARCH LABORATORIES** At night the façade comes alive with a collage of colours that gives the building a strong presence, making it immediately recognizable on the Biberach campus.

8

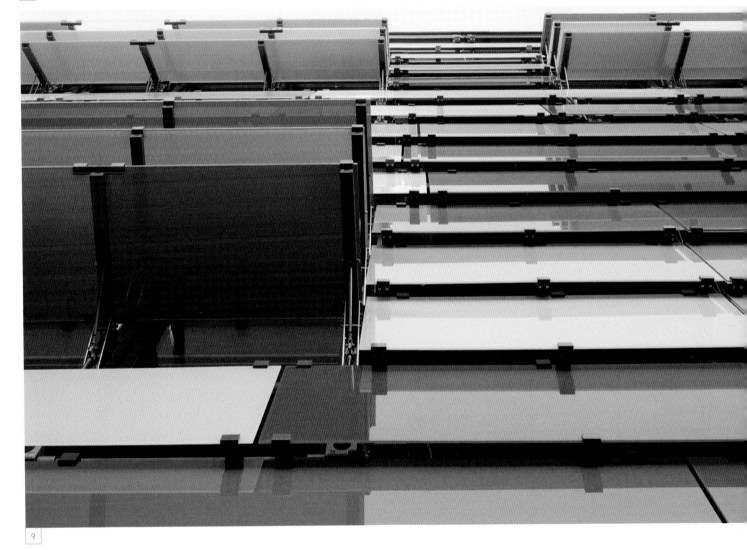

9

7 | **FIRE AND POLICE STATION**, Berlin, Germany, 2004. The glazing is printed with an opaque enamel in a reverse dot pattern; the dots are clear, and it is the background that is printed.

8 | **FIRE AND POLICE STATION** At night the building is at its most dramatic, a patchwork of red and green. Only on closer inspection does one perceive the open joints between the panels of colour.

9 | **FIRE AND POLICE STATION** When located in front of windows on the inner façade, the coloured panels are operable louvres printed with an 85% screen dot. Elsewhere they are opaque and act as cladding.

1 **SPA BATH**, Bad Elster, Germany, 1999. A ceiling of adjustable coloured glass louvres creates a cheerful enclosure for the large swimming hall and can be adjusted with the changing seasons.

Behnisch and Partner is an international practice, with offices in Stuttgart in Germany, and in the United States. Its architecture is characterized by transparency, lightness, and commitment to energy conservation.

A colourful glazed swimming-pool hall is the centrepiece of a 1999 spa renovation in Bad Elster, Germany, near the Czech border. The approximately 22 x 22m (70 x 70ft) steel and glass pavilion occupies a previously under-utilized courtyard in the spa complex and has as its backdrop uninterrupted views of the existing 19th-century Jugendstil buildings. In the plane of the roof the architects have made bold use of coloured glazing. An external roof canopy and an internal ceiling of colourful operable glass louvres, designed in collaboration with the Berlin artist Erich Wiesner, create a horizontal enclosure for the pool hall and a constantly changing play of light and colour that varies with the weather.

The louvres are suspended on a white steel structure, which also supports an outer layer of clear insulating glass that provides protection from the elements. Because the louvres can be adjusted, they can be used to modulate light and solar gain: they can be closed completely at night or in winter, and remain open during the warm weather of the summer. The louvres' upper surface is printed with a 45 percent white frit to reduce the impact of the sun, while the underside is coated with a collage of colours – blue, yellow, green, and red – screen-printed onto the glass, creating graduated tones that make playful reflections on the surface of the pools and on the surrounding white-tiled patios. The glass, being overhead, is both toughened and laminated to provide additional safety.

2

2 **SPA BATH** Reds, blues, greens, and yellows of varying hues and transparencies are printed on the inner sides of the glazing, which is then laminated.

3 **SPA BATH** A cloudlike motif printed across the louvres adds further interest and variety, and can easily be mistaken for the real clouds floating overhead.

3

This Hamburg-based architectural practice has been fortunate to work with a manufacturing company that has been producing glass for artists for years. The architects were able to draw from this wealth of experience and benefit from a team accustomed to the demands of artists.

Medium Architects' inventive use of coloured glass in their Hamburg Law Library exploits the potential of this medium to create a rich and varied building, both inside and out. The coloured glass in the façade makes the building dynamic and welcoming both by day and by night. Three of the façades consist of horizontal glazing panels, about half of which are clear and the rest are four tones of yellow and amber. The chosen colours have both energy and calm. The coloured panels appear to be distributed randomly on the façade; however, their positioning was in fact studied carefully to create privacy where needed, to highlight particular views, and to create a working environment with a variety of moods. The exterior of the glass is etched with parallel lines, some horizontal and some vertical, which modulate the transparency of the glazing. This increases privacy, and playfully alters the views out.

The glazed yet windowless south elevation has a different treatment. Along with the original library and a 19th-century villa, the southern façade forms the fourth side of an urban square where students gather. Stylized tree imagery in green and yellow is incorporated into a glazed cavity wall to create a "park" for the plaza. The façade is a cavity system with two layers of glass, 20cm (8in) apart, that serves as a thermal collector, allowing hot air to rise within the cavity. Six different green tones and a few yellow bands are printed on the interior layer of glass. The exterior layer is sandblasted with a pattern of natural organic shapes. The combination of these two layers of glass, which in sunlight allows moving shadows to appear on the inner layer, evokes the experience of sunlight falling through a canopy of trees.

1

2

1   **HAMBURG LAW LIBRARY**, Germany, 2004. The south elevation is a double-skinned cavity façade. The outer layer is printed with tree imagery, which reflects changing patterns onto the inner glazing.

2   **HAMBURG LAW LIBRARY** Opaque strips of yellow glazing offset rectangular panels of six green tones in a subtle play of colours. Etched horizontal lines add texture to the glazing.

3

4

5

3 **HAMBURG LAW LIBRARY** The street façades make a bolder use of colour in amber and yellow tones. At night the building is like a beacon, advertising its 24-hour opening schedule.

4 **HAMBURG LAW LIBRARY** Amber glazing is positioned at floor level to create privacy in the reading areas; glass at eye level is clear. Colour is used to create a calm atmosphere within the interior.

5 **HAMBURG LAW LIBRARY** The etched coloured glazing provides just enough transparency to enable passers by to perceive the building's occupants without intruding on their privacy.

Laminated glass comprises two layers of glass bonded together by a flexible plastic or resin interlayer that ensures the glass does not break into pieces if fractured (as commonly seen in windscreen glass). The three methods in use are known as poured, UV-cured, and dry lamination.

For years it has been possible to pigment the liquid resin that is used to make poured laminated glass – turning the glass almost any colour, transparent, or translucent. But this process has not been widely exploited, perhaps because each piece is hand-made and the process is not perceived as suitable for mass production.

In recent years a large global glass company has patented a more mechanized system, developing a method of colouring the dry PVB (polyvinyl butyral) material that is used to laminate glass. Up to four sheets of these coloured interlayers can be mixed together, turning the range of nine base colours into a wide variety of possible tones. In this section we see this system used by a number of adventurous architects, for whom the use of colour in their design and execution has been central to their overall aesthetic.

Pigmented laminated glass offers the opportunity to create rich and multicoloured glass or restrained, quiet colours. Recently a system called EVA (ethylene vinyl acetate) has become more widely used. This creates much greater flexibility of lamination and allows the creation of many state-of-the-art features. It has enabled the inclusion of different materials, including LED lights, inside the laminated glass panels, as well as allowing the use of textured glass and even photovoltaic cells (*see* Glossary p.185).

TOP & ABOVE **CHRISTCHURCH ART GALLERY**, Christchurch, New Zealand, 2003, 100 x 15m (330 x 50ft). Melbourne-based architectural practice The Buchan Group designed this long, curved and tilted Sculpture Wall, with 2,500 glass panels facing the sun. It is made up of 11 different types of reflective and low-emission coatings, carefully orchestrated to create continually shifting colours – more transparent at the base and more reflective at the top.

ABOVE **THE WESTIN**, Time Square, New York, USA, 2003: designed by Arquitectonica. There are 21 different types of glass panels in this building, made up in a range of copper, gold, and rust colours contrasting with silver, blue, purple, and aqua, all with reflectivity values to sustain the colour scheme of the monolithic walls.

TOP RIGHT, MIDDLE RIGHT & BOTTOM RIGHT
MAESTRO NICOLAU OFFICE BUILDING, Barcelona, Spain, 2004: by Fermin Vazquez of b720 Architects. Forty rows of laminated glass in ten sections, graduated from red to yellow, create external venetian blinds to filter out solar radiation. The panels get increasingly close together as they

go higher up the building, with the absence of frames allowing the colours to become a progressive gradation of tones. Although the colour is a dominant feature from the exterior, even casting colours onto the pavement, it is only marginally perceived from inside the building.

David Adjaye's Idea Store, completed in 2004 as part of a programme of library replacements in London's East End borough of Tower Hamlets, represents a total rethink of the concept of a public library. Adjaye has taken Alsop's Peckham Library (see pp.48–9) and streamlined it for the local high street. Like Peckham, the building is instantly recognizable by day and reads as a beacon by night. Coloured glass is used on the two visible façades to make a statement about accessibility and transparency. Eye-catching panels of coloured glazing 4.5m (15ft) tall by 60cm (24in) wide fade from blue to green to yellow as they march around the façade.

With the Idea Store, Adjaye has transformed the curtain-wall cladding usually found on large office buildings by applying it to a small, two-storey building and adding colour. The range of colours is achieved with pigmented laminated glass. Six base colours are combined in different ways to achieve six different colours on the façade, each panel using two to four of the base colours. The entire range includes nine base colours to achieve numerous shades. Thermally, the coloured glazing panels perform slightly better than clear glazing.

From the inside the changing pattern of colours contributes to a sense of enclosure, and enlivens the otherwise drab exterior views of a housing estate tower block. The concept behind the Idea Store is to demystify the notion of the public library by using a retail model to attract a consumer-minded public. Visual display of information is an important part of the new concept – made possible and enhanced by the transparency of the façades. Adjaye's choice of coloured glazing is an appropriate response to this rebranding of the public library and is being replicated in the second Idea Store in London's Whitechapel, due for completion in late 2005.

1 | **IDEA STORE (LIBRARY)**, London, England, 2004. This shows how effective the use of colour is at night, especially for such buildings as this that seek to be after-hours landmarks.

2 | **IDEA STORE (LIBRARY)** The effect of the coloured glass is not pervasive or invasive of the interior space. Rather it adds interest, rhythm, and colour to a relatively stark interior.

3 | **IDEA STORE (LIBRARY)** The daytime exterior image shows the contribution to the streetscape that is provided by this simple but potent use of coloured glass.

1

The Peckham Library in London has been a much-publicized building in the UK, winning the prestigious Stirling Prize upon completion in 2000 and arousing the controversy that its architect, Will Alsop, seems always to create. Whereas most people like buildings to be firmly rooted in the ground, Alsop's buildings often look as if they are about to walk off, as happens in *Alice in Wonderland*, just as you get to the front door. Alsop has an equally defiant relationship with colour, often challenging restrained, northern European sensibilities with a bold and assertive palette.

At the Peckham Library Alsop uses both reflective and transparent coloured glass to dynamic effect. The north and south façades of the library are clad with floor-to-floor clear and multicoloured glazing panels. During the day the yellow cladding reads as prominent bands of colour; but at night the panels withdraw, and the coloured glass of the stairwells and the double-height spaces become the dominant feature. Inside, multicoloured shadows enliven the children's reading room.

There is nothing subtle about Alsop's use of colour at the Peckham Library, and its contribution to the landscape is more of a clarion call than an aesthetic stimulation. But the result is a building that everyone remembers, and that people want to visit and enjoy. Alsop is unequivocal in his condemnation of the passive and the inactive, the tepid and the lukewarm. His buildings are an assertion of a philosophy, or perhaps a psychology, that demands response and reaction, and that continues to inspire and to stimulate.

1 **PECKHAM LIBRARY**, London, England, 2000. This daylight view shows the coloured glass making a simple abstract composition that interacts with the reflections of neighbouring buildings.

2 **PECKHAM LIBRARY** The amber, pink, and yellow colours shown here can be seen in picture 1 at the base of the building. This shows the effect of the coloured glass from inside.

3 **PECKHAM LIBRARY** During the evening the colour composition changes as the cladding panels recede (see the yellow vertical bands on the right) and the back-lit glazing panels become dominant.

2

3

The Brazilian architect Brunete Fraccaroli is noted for her bold, liberated use of glass and colour. Much of her work involves leisure and hospitality environments executed in dramatic tones, sometimes using graduated film that is laminated inside glass to create fluid, curved forms from flat surfaces.

The project featured, a Japanese barbecue restaurant in Brazil, has been created within an existing older property. As befits a barbecue restaurant, part of the intention was to create an interior space that was relaxed and comfortable and that felt closely connected to the exterior environment. Rather than create a classic conservatory, or even a contemporary type of atrium, Fraccaroli has created an unusual, striking space. She has installed big diagonal steel girders to support a large, north-facing, sloping glazed ceiling. Instead of treating the girders as mere engineering elements to be somehow disguised or expressed as steel, she has drawn them to

the attention of customers as they enter the space by cladding them in purple PVB-laminated reflecting mirror.

By this bold strategy, the beams are no longer a minimalist supporting structure for the required enclosing glazing, nor plaster-clad white boxes that challenge the glass yet add nothing. Instead they have become a central part of the form, the colour, and the experience of the space, and they begin to merge with the clear, sloping external glazing.

In contrast to all these angular modernist shapes and the harshness of the mirrored steel beams, all the furniture is made from rough wood, scattered with soft cushions, and there is a ceramic floor.

To complete the theme and the experience, on the back wall of the bar Fraccaroli has installed 750 glass bottles filled with purple liquid. At night the bottles are lit with fibre-optic light sources, creating a soft glowing effect as they reflect off the beams' angled surfaces.

2

1 **JAPANESE BARBECUE RESTAURANT,**
Sao Paolo, Brazil, 2004.
Large girders become integrated central parts of a themed hospitality interior by being clad in pigmented mirror.

2 **JAPANESE BARBECUE RESTAURANT** From close up the mirror appears to reduce the mass of the structural beams by reflecting light.

3 **JAPANESE BARBECUE RESTAURANT** A total of 750 glass bottles filled with purple liquid complete the theme of this restaurant.

3

James Carpenter has been working in the interface between architecture, glass, and art for most of his career. He started out as a sculpture and glass art student, then became a teacher, then a visiting artist at Corning Glass, and finally worked with Steuben Glass, a division of Corning specializing in decorated and moulded glass. It is this unique combination of working with major glass manufacturers, and at the same time pursuing his own sculptural interests, that has given Carpenter an unusual understanding of the technology involved in glass manufacture, as well an extraordinary artistic sensibility that is based on a pure architectural aesthetic.

In the late 1970s Carpenter set up his practice, James Carpenter Design Associates, which has been called upon ever since by clients and architects to undertake specialist interventions in major architectural projects that require his unusual mix of vision, talent, knowledge, and experience.

1

2

1 **MOIRÉ STAIR TOWER**, Deutsche Post, Bonn, Germany, 2002. This three-storey tower is made almost entirely of glass. A screen pattern on the laminated walls shows blue rectangles facing into the stairwell.

2 **MOIRÉ STAIR TOWER** Located on a landing between levels is a balcony that presents views of the landscape and river, framed by the grid of rectangles and the strange optical effects of the pattern.

3 **MOIRÉ STAIR TOWER** From the building's exterior the effect of a vast field of small equally spaced mirrors pixellates the surroundings and the sky into thousands of tiny separated images.

4 **MOIRÉ STAIR TOWER** The triangular form ensures that each wall is reflected in the adjacent wall, creating multiple layers of patterns merging and interacting with each other.

The Deutche Post Moiré Stair Tower is a classic Carpenter project. Led by his senior designer and long-time associate Richard Kress, this huge permanent art "installation" is actually a relatively modest three-storey adjunct to the 240-m (790-ft) high corporate headquarters designed by Chicago architects Murphy Jahn.

The rectangular grid pattern on the three exterior glass walls is made up of mirror facing out, and bright blue facing in. From outside, the effect of the myriad tiny mirrors is to create a flickering silver image that sparkles in sunlight and is always slightly moving. Inside, the space becomes quite surreal: the stair treads are glass, and the grid patterns behave like an exercise in perspective, streaking away to vanishing points while concurrently merging with the reflected images of the adjacent wall, crossing over in a huge moiré pattern of different shades of blue. The result is an experience of total immersion – installation art at its best, and permanent too.

3

4

London's new Home Office building, by the Terry Farrell Partnership, is filled with art, but the exterior coloured glass features inevitably command the most attention.

From the outset the architect developed a detailed overall art strategy, which involved creating vitrines (floor-to-ceiling glass boxes) along the street that could house some form of art object, and also using glass in the cladding and the exterior of the building. Since the client was the UK Home Office, the government Department of Culture, Media and Sport became involved in the selection of an artist for the glazing. Liam Gillick, a nominee for the prestigious Turner Prize, was selected because his work involves transparency and colour and also because of his experience of working collaboratively.

Originally a concrete canopy was planned to go along the top of the building on the main street façade, but Gillick suggested making the canopy of glass. Because cleaning cradles have to move up and down the building,

an aperture in the canopy was needed. Instead of being an obstacle, this became a design opportunity: some panels are vertical, creating the passageway required and adding another variation to the way coloured light is reflected around the building. The canopy has its greatest impact during the day, causing bands of colour to be reflected along the street. Gillick's proposal for the vitrines was that each should have a series of coloured glass fins, creating a feature that works both inside and outside. The vitrines come into their own at night, when the rich colours create vibrant rainbows of vertical bands.

It is the simplicity and the cost-effectiveness of the whole concept that is so striking. This is not painting on glass. It is a simple and straightforward way of incorporating colour into architecture and into the streetscape. That it has an elevating effect on the environment is undeniable, and the architect felt it enhanced the architecture: a good example of art and architecture working together.

1

2

1 **HOME OFFICE BUILDING**, London, England, 2005. The use of brightly coloured glazing in the canopy, designed in collaboration with the artist Liam Gillick, makes an otherwise restrained building stand out in the streetscape.

2 **HOME OFFICE BUILDING** The coloured glass canopy at roof level uses horizontal and vertical glazing panels that reflect light in different ways onto the façade and the pavement, and even onto nearby buildings.

3 **HOME OFFICE BUILDING** Special vitrines along the ground floor glazing are defined by vertical fins of multicoloured glass. The effect on the interior during daylight and the exterior at night is bright and cheerful.

PALAIS DES CONGRÈS,
Montreal, Canada, 2003.
Strong colours give immediate
identity to a project whose brief
was to revitalize a neighbourhood
between the historic centre
and the city's downtown.

Few architects inhabit the interface between art and architecture with such drama and consistency as Hal Ingberg. A native of Montreal, he has studied in both Montreal and Los Angeles and worked in London. A Canadian Prix de Rome winner, he started his own practice in 1999. By playing with colour, reflections, and transparency, Ingberg creates dynamic multi-dimensional works that range from sculpture to architecture.

In 2003 Ingberg exhibited his landscape installation "Coloured Reflections" at the International Garden Festival in Quebec (*see* pp.58–9). Large, green, semi-reflective glass panels created shimmering images of trees, merging reality and reflection, upon two-dimensional planes. It was hugely popular. For the 2004 Biennale de Montréal, Ingberg created "Beacon" – a golden glass tower that stood in the centre of Montreal's Place des Arts. This work also plays with reflections and transparency, so that reality and image interact.

Ingberg's merging of art and architecture led to his nomination as consultant architect for the renovation and expansion of Montreal's Palais des Congrès, the city's convention centre. His bold proposal of transparent multicoloured glass panes was controversial, but he achieved his objective – to create an urban icon whose primary space is dramatically washed in a psychedelic bath of projected, coloured light. At the same time he created a powerful vista from the exterior, which is equally dynamic during the day and at night, and celebrates this vital hub of city life.

While the Palais des Congrès is spectacular and animated, Ingberg's other projects are in great contrast. Each so serene due to the careful choice of colour, designed to accentuate the surroundings that merge with the reflective plane of the glass. Their vibrancy comes from the fact that they are continually changing, as they respond to every movement in the environment.

1

2

3

PALAIS DES CONGRÈS
2 Transparent, coloured glass and mirrored stainless steel create a dizzying kaleidoscope of reflections along a pedestrian path through the complex, attracting visitors to experience the building in differing light conditions.

PALAIS DES CONGRÈS
3 Projected coloured light is a trademark of this large urban complex, which houses an exhibition space as well as retail activities.

4 **"COLOURED REFLECTIONS"** (temporary installation), Reford Gardens, Grand-Métis, Quebec, Canada, 2003. A standing triangle of reflective green glass blends reflections of the forest with the forest itself.

5 **"COLOURED REFLECTIONS"** The installation enclosed three birch trees, creating a space where one could contemplate the forest from inside the triangle, looking out into the trees beyond.

6 **"COLOURED REFLECTIONS"** At different times of day, depending on the light and the angle of the sun, the glass would change from reflective to transparent and everything inbetween, even sometimes seeming to disappear.

7 **"COLOURED REFLECTIONS"** The installation is most effective as a surprise encounter, where there is an air of mystery and illusion. It was extremely popular with visitors to the garden festival.

4

5

6

7

8

9

10

11

8 **"BEACON"** (temporary installation), Montreal, Canada, 2004. The panels reflect the clouds in the sky. From different angles the installation challenges perceptions of scale.

9 **"BEACON"** This shows the internal view when the tower is entered. On cloudy days the glass becomes an opaque mirror, but in sunlight a gold-tinted cityscape can be seen outside.

10 **"BEACON"** The installation playfully reflects passers-by and the surrounding city environment, encouraging visitors to explore and enjoy the public space.

11 **"BEACON"** The 6.4-m (21-ft) tall triangular tower, made of semi-reflective gold panels, occupies a pedestal at the base of public stairs in Montreal's Place des Arts.

The building industry has been using applied films on glass for years. Film has been used as a safety feature, to convert plain or toughened glass into a laminated glass, and as a solar reduction device. The technology of making films that will adhere successfully and reliably to glass is well proven and extremely sophisticated.

The technology to print digitally onto film has now also become widespread, and even more recently the ability to print in white onto film has become possible, though this is far from common yet. However, the potential of these materials and their possible applications has barely been touched, let alone exploited. This may be due to a natural suspicion that the material will deteriorate too quickly to be satisfactory, and partly because often architects do not regard this level of detail as part of their brief.

In reality the range of options is enormous, and it is the flexibility of use inherent in film applications that is one of its major advantages. The material is not expensive, and so it brings with it the option to rebrand an environment at very low cost, and with no structural alterations. In the fast-moving world of re-imaging and of creating stimulating environments for employees, this type of flexibility can be a huge plus.

In addition to coloured films and to digitally printed film there is also dichroic film. We have illustrated this here, but, although the product is easily available, it is not so easily found with the optimum adhesive for glass applications; the packaging and retail industries have taken over this product and it is no longer in production for its glass applications, although this may change. The effects of film on glass can sometimes be extreme, and it may well be a little explosive for the average planner or consumer.

ABOVE **HOLMES PLACE HEALTH CLUB, COLOGNE**, Germany, 2002: by ORMS Architects. Film is remarkably durable. These sliding doors have been transformed into bold features in the interior by the simple addition of transparent yellow adhesive film.

ABOVE **HOLMES PLACE HEALTH CLUB, COLOGNE**
Seen in sunlight, the etched film encloses the space,
softening the interior light, whereas the coloured film throws
bands of bright colour onto the interior white surfaces.

TOP **HOLMES PLACE HEALTH CLUB, COLOGNE**
From the outside, as shown in this night-time picture, the
bands of blue and yellow film create a strong horizontal
architectural feature.

ABOVE **HOLMES PLACE HEALTH CLUB, VIENNA**,
Austria, 2001: by ORMS Architects. This interior picture
shows the mixed use of transparent coloured film
and etched film.

Two very different projects by the Dutch-based architectural practice UN Studio, both completed in 2004, use dichroic film in their façades to create eye-catching buildings that change according to time of day and point of view. In both cases – one the refurbishment of a shopping mall in Seoul, South Korea, and the other a new office complex in Almere, The Netherlands – the dynamic use of colour renders the buildings instantly distinctive. Both projects treat the exterior envelope as a single surface; the buildings are swathed in a play of changing colour that strikes a balance between visibility and subtlety.

The La Defense office complex in Almere uses dichroic film incorporated into glazed cladding panels to cloak the internal courtyards of the 23,000sq-m (250,000 sq-ft) project in an effervescent rainbow of colour. Some of the glazing acts as cladding and some as windows. The cladding, with higher light levels in front of the glass, tends to act in its reflective mode, giving off the red and gold colours we see in the exterior pictures. The glazing that forms the windows changes as the viewer moves, from its main transparent colour of pure deep blue into purples, crimsons, and subtle colours inbetween. The reflective manifestation creates a play of colourful shadows in the courtyard, whereas the office interiors are bathed in diffused coloured light.

Commissioned to rejuvenate Seoul's upmarket Galleria shopping centre, UN Studio responded by wrapping the entire structure with 4,330 glass discs, each attached to a metal substructure on the existing façade. Each 850-mm (34-in) disc is back-lit with an LED fitting, and consists of two layers of sandblasted laminated glass incorporating a dichroic foil. During the day the discs glow in a range of pale colours from green to amber, depending on the light. At night a rolling effect of changing colours is achieved by the computer-programmed LED fittings – a lighting concept designed jointly with Arup Lighting.

1 **LA DEFENSE OFFICE BUILDING**, Almere, The Netherlands, 2004. The model of the building helps in navigating images 2–5. The dramatic use of dichroic film is confined within the courtyards created by the interlocking buildings.

2 **LA DEFENSE OFFICE BUILDING** Viewing the building from directly in front we can see how some film, used as cladding, is reflecting gold and red, while other areas, illuminated from behind, show a transmitted blue light.

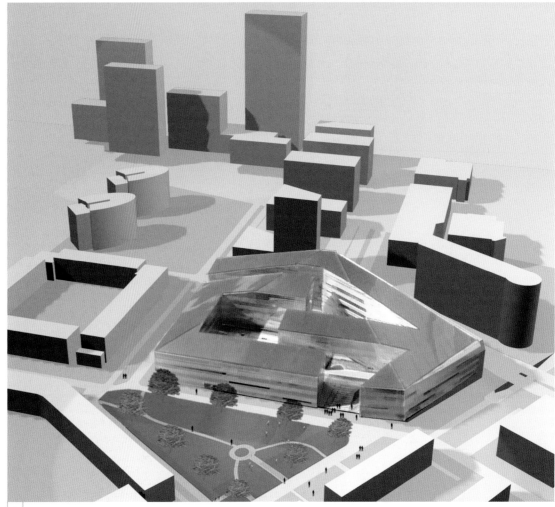

1

3

4

5

3 **LA DEFENSE OFFICE BUILDING** From inside we see across a courtyard to the cladding opposite that is reflecting greens and golds, whereas the glazing through which we are looking, illuminated by daylight, is showing blue mixed with red because it is viewed from an angle.

4 **LA DEFENSE OFFICE BUILDING** At night the cladding panels lose their colour almost entirely, while the glazing, back-lit by internal light, shines blue, moving towards purple as the angle of vision increases.

5 **LA DEFENSE OFFICE BUILDING** This shows how the interlocking walls of the buildings create a series of converging diagonals and angles, emphasizing the changing nature of the coloured material.

6 GALLERIA HALL WEST,
Seoul, South Korea, 2004.
4,330 discs, made up of two layers
of low-iron glass, laminated
together with the dichroic film
inbetween, are suspended
from an aluminium structure.

7 GALLERIA HALL WEST
In daylight the discs
shimmer with iridescent
colours reflecting through
their etched surfaces.

8 GALLERIA HALL WEST
At night each disc is lit
with an LED-light source, which
can be centrally controlled to
create different effects and
patterns across the entire
outer skin of the building.

6

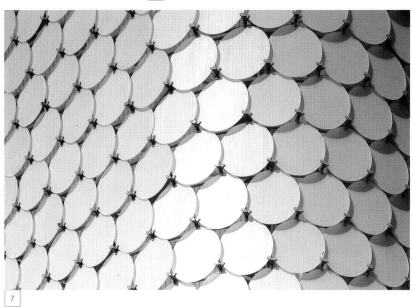

7

8

1 PEABODY TRUST SILVERTOWN HOUSING, London, England, 2004. At every hour of the day the Peabody flats reflect differing light conditions, creating a mysterious and ethereal effect on the façade.

Niall McLaughlin is fascinated with light – as he says, "combing it, diffusing it, storing it, colouring it, reflecting it, dulling it, and changing its speed". It is therefore no surprise to find him exploiting the properties of film in two recent projects – one in the exterior façade of social housing for the Peabody Trust, the other an interiors project in London's Covent Garden.

On a post-industrial site in East London McLaughlin has built a block of 12 apartments, for which his initial concept was a series of packing crates clad in an inexpensive industrial sheeting. The south-facing street elevation of the three-storey buildings is clad in bespoke units that incorporate dichroic film between layers of aluminium and cast glass. The triple-glazed units, prefabricated in Dublin, consist of an exterior face of roughcast glass, a second layer of horizontal strips of polycarbonate with dichroic film, and a rear panel of aluminium, also faced with dichroic film, offset from the

film in front. The alternating position of the film inside the cladding unit multiplies the range of colours that filter through the cast-glass front layer, creating a shimmering effect on the façade that varies with the time of day and the weather. This effect is not seen inside the apartments because the backs of the cladding panels are opaque.

For a business psychology consulting firm's offices, McLaughlin used fixed and sliding glass screens with digitally printed film to create privacy, while allowing light to penetrate the centre of the floor plan. The adhesive film is transparent and has been printed with vertical wavering lines, like flattened interlocking sine waves, and applied to one side of the glass. The architects want the screens to "fizz" with a dynamic effect as the different colours and patterns slide across one another. The interior is illuminated with a subtle rainbow of colours.

1

2

2 **PEABODY TRUST SILVERTOWN**

HOUSING Inexpensive dichroic film is used to enhance the appeal of low-cost housing, giving it a fresh and contemporary look, which is particularly appealing because it is constantly changing.

3 **PEABODY TRUST SILVERTOWN**

HOUSING Strips of dichroic film, set within the cladding panels at different distances from the exterior glazing, create ribbons of colour that glow within the façade.

3

4

5

6

7

4 **YSC LTD**, Floral Street, Covent Garden, London, England, 2005. Sliding glass panels with printed adhesive film allow flexible use of space for a business psychology consultancy.

5 **YSC LTD** As the coloured glass panels slide in front of one another different colour combinations appear, animating what would otherwise be a lifeless interior corridor.

6 **YSC LTD** The intensity of the colours is such that they reflect into the adjacent spaces, creating dynamic work areas whose degree of privacy is adjustable according to need.

7 **YSC LTD** Subtle wavering lines printed on the adhesive film give a three-dimensional quality to the coloured panels that is reminiscent of Op Art.

I am this far advanced & rea

GREEN LAKE

Artists on the whole have a different perspective from architects when designing glass. Mostly their brief is to design a specific feature or to create a localized effect in a building, as we see from the following images, while architects tend to want to add something to the entire fabric of the structure.

This section of the book is divided into five basic techniques, two more than in the Architecture section. It would be wrong to imagine that the artists chosen to represent each technique always use the same one; some might use enamelled glass for certain projects, laminated antique for others, and for still others a combination of both, with the final result being slumped and sandblasted. The changes that have occurred in this art form are reflected in the variety of grand and small-scale projects.

Several major glass art studios in the world specialize in the manufacture of glass designs. These have been in the forefront of the revolution in techniques, expanding their facilities, making new technology available, and keeping up with ever-changing methods. Yet some artists prefer to retain complete control over the execution of their work, and develop the facilities and manpower to manufacture their designs in their own factory or workshop.

Artists with little or no experience in glass increasingly are being commissioned to design projects. Yet this is not a modern phenomenon: Joshua Reynolds, Frank Lloyd Wright, Edward Burne-Jones, Antonio Gaudí, Josef Albers, Henri Matisse, Marc Chagall, and John Piper, to name just the obvious, all designed glass windows. They all experienced the medium as one of the most satisfying they had ever encountered. Chagall, at 90, claimed he was living to so great an age because he had only started to work in glass in his 70s.

Glass is profoundly different from other media because – as each artist states as if it has never been said before – it is about working with light. And it is hard to get more fundamental than that first requirement of all visual aesthetics: light.

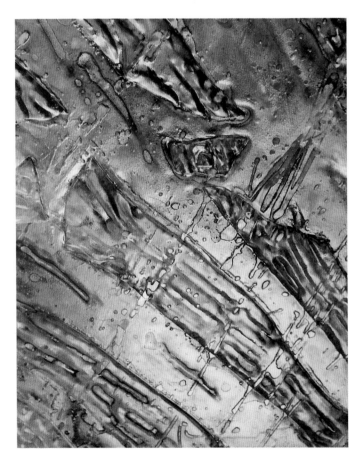

PREVIOUS PAGE **GREENWOOD LIBRARY**, Seattle, Washington, USA, 2004: by Fernanda d'Agostino, an installation artist working in video, bronze, stone, and glass. This window is a double-glazed unit; both layers of glass, executed with screen-printed and airbrushed enamels, create floating images on a textured background.

ABOVE LEFT **SYNAGOGUE**, Jerusalem, Israel, 2002: by Mira Maylor. The detail shows a surface texture created by slumping glass. This panel has also been painted with cold colours.

ABOVE **"VISION'S NUCLEUS"**, private residence, New York, USA, 2001: by Eric Hilton. This piece, carved by sandblasting, shows how an artist such as Hilton can turn plain glass into a sculptured, three-dimensional form, and how coloured glass can be introduced to contrast with the white surround.

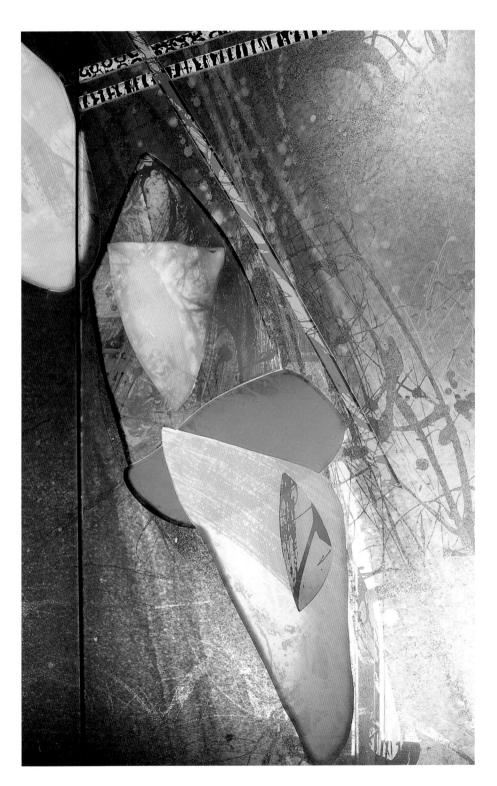

ABOVE **BAKER MCKENZIE CORPORATE HQ**, London, England, 2003: by Graham Jones. Detail from a large screen showing screen-printed enamels, plus acid-etching, plus green and yellow antique glass pieces bonded to the surface.

ABOVE RIGHT **LEIF HÖEGH & CO CORPORATE HQ**, Oslo, Norway, 2005: by Espen Tollefsen. Digitally printed film on glass creates images on an office partitioning that are visible from both sides.

Today we tend to associate the expression "stained glass" with leaded glass. In fact the term simply refers to the act of staining glass – painting the glass with vitreous enamels and firing them so that they become part of the glass. The process has been a central part of the tradition of stained glass for a thousand years.

In this section we explore the way in which many artists have moved away, not only from using leaded glass, but also from using mouth-blown coloured glass. Increasingly they are using enamel paints on float glass to create the colour on the glass, with the objective that, once fired, the product can function as a standard piece of structural glazing.

Although enamels have specific requirements, owing to the firing process, that make them different from other kinds of painting media, there are only three major methods of applying the enamels. They can be painted, airbrushed, or screen-printed, though within these broad categories lie many tricks and techniques that individual craftspeople and artists use to achieve different effects.

Vitreous enamels come in both transparent and opaque form. The transparent colours make up only a small spectrum and are sensitive to heat, duration of firing, and even moisture. Transparent enamels are often used on etched glass, making the colours brighter and the glass translucent rather than transparent.

Architects have been using "fritted" glass for some years now (*see* pp.20–21). Enamelled glass is the same material. It is this convergence of methodology that makes the opportunity for collaboration far more straightforward.

ABOVE **"SYMFONIA"**, Oslo National University Hospital, Norway, 2000, 8 x 20m (26 x 65ft): by Odd Tandberg. This window is made with transparent screen-printed enamels on the inside of the exterior double-glazing.

OPPOSITE TOP LEFT **ENTRANCE TO JAMES COOK UNIVERSITY HOSPITAL**, Middlesbrough, England, 2002: by Bridget Jones. These panels are double-glazed units, screen-printed with enamels and with acid-etched abstract forms.

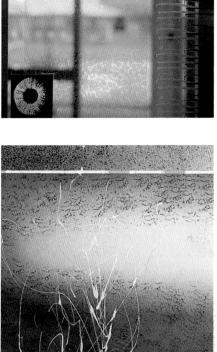

ENTRANCE TO JAMES COOK UNIVERSITY HOSPITAL All the surface treatments are on the insides of the units, allowing for easy cleaning. This includes the antique glass squares of "sea urchins" that are laminated to the toughened-glass panels.

ABOVE **"TIME & TIDES"**, 22nd St Bayonne Station, New Jersey, USA, 2004: by Kenneth Leap. In total 15 panels of 12-mm (0.5-in) toughened glass have been screen-printed with images of the town in several colours and layers, with dichroic glass and bevelled strips.

ABOVE **"AQUA"**, Kuwait Embassy, Ottawa, Canada, 2001: by Sarah Hall. The panel, created with sandblasting and hand-painted and airbrushed enamels, evokes the colours and textures of a tropical seascape.

Martin Donlin graduated from the Swansea Architectural Glass School in 1987. Despite training as a stained-glass artist, he soon found himself doing commissions that involved float glass – external balustrades, large floor-to-ceiling mirrors, planar walls, and curved glass canopies.

Since his first large project, in 1989, Donlin has been creating projects in the UK and abroad, mostly working with large panels of float glass that integrate easily into the form and structure of the building. He was one of the very first UK-based artists to explore the possibilities of screen-printed enamels on glass. Like many glass artists, he likes to mix techniques, including different types of etching, painting, airbrushing, and printing with enamels, as well as using antique glass bonded to float and so on.

Donlin is an accomplished illustrator and likes to incorporate images, text, or forms that relate to the site and the specific function or context of the building. The Manchester bridge shown below uses small detailed graphics lifted from the history of the area, while the Liverpool cinema, with its vast torn ticket reference, has hundreds of intricate details that can be seen only when standing next to the glass, including a history of the Empire Theatre and details of famous performers. Donlin makes the incorporation of these items seem effortless. The glass of the Southampton cinema (*see* p.80) is filled with references to film reels and other film imagery.

Donlin's gift is that he sticks to strong, bold solutions. His designs work as simple, vivid forms from a distance, and yet reveal intriguing detail as the viewer draws near. His work is not complex to construct, but every detail is planned with great care. The result is cost-efficient and pleasing to all those involved.

1

1 TIB STREET BRIDGE LINK, Manchester, England, 1999, 18 x 2.2m (59 x 7ft). Built in collaboration with the architects Stephenson Bell, this bridge has toughened glass, screen-printed with opaque and transparent enamels.

2 TIB STREET BRIDGE LINK, seen from inside, showing something of the detailed graphics, maps, and text that viewers can enjoy as they pass along the bridge.

3 EMPIRE THEATRE, Liverpool, England, 2002, 6mm x 15m (0.2in x 50ft). Architect: Ellis Williams. The exterior view of this cinema, decorated wtih enamelled toughened glass, is distinctly different from that of the interior, where many detailed items appear – adding to the texture as well as to the narrative content.

2

4

4 **HARBOUR LIGHTS CINEMA**, Southampton, England, 1999, 12 x 2.4m (40 x 8ft). Architect: Burrell Foley Fischer. This glass art piece forms the south elevation of the building. More and more details relating to film and film projection emerge as one enters into the enclosed space.

5 **BREWERY LANE**, Bridgend, Wales, 2004, 150sqm (1600sqft). Architect: Wigley Fox Partnership. This office development has been transformed into a fabulous night-time landmark by the powerful vertical bands of colour. In detail, thousands of tiny human figures can be seen throughout the glass panels.

5

6

6 **HOLYWOOD ARCHES HOSPITAL**, Belfast, Northern Ireland, 2004, 5 x 15m (16 x 50ft). Architect: Todd Architects. The glass is printed with images of herbs and other plants that relate to the healing role of the building. The work changes as the light varies.

7 **HOLYWOOD ARCHES HOSPITAL** Interior view. In contrast to other projects, the work becomes more abstract as you approach the glass, while from a distance the actual images are more distinct.

7

Washington State has established itself as the centre of the Hot Glass Studio Movement of the United States, and Tacoma, with its newly opened Glass Museum, is at the heart of this movement. The state has recently commissioned several artists to create public glass art projects in support of this growing identity (*see* also Linda Beaumont's project at Sea-Tac Airport, pp.84–5).

Stuart Keeler and Michael Machnic work both independently and as a team, producing architectural public artworks. Their brief in this project, the Tacoma Convention Center, encompassed more than just the glass membrane – it was the designs for the glass envelope of the building that became the dominant force in their overall concept to express the history of the area, working collaboratively with the architect to enhance the space.

Tacoma at one time was synonymous with the timber industry, the region being entirely forested with old-growth trees. From this derives the ghostly images of five trunks of old-growth timber, forms that inevitably pull the eye upward. Being printed with a large-scale dot screen, the images have become transparent and ethereal. This works as a contrast to the printed contour maps that are made up of images of Mount Rainier, a volcano on the edge of the city, rising out of the flatlands of the valley and often shrouded in cloud and surrounded by snow and ice. Thus the entire façade of Tacoma Convention Center is covered in abstracted images of the mountain as seen from above. These are printed in two colours that are slightly misregistered – a translucent white and a rich transparent gold. The gold creates a tonal bridge with the interior wood finishes, which are themselves a crucial part of Keeler and Machnic's concept for the building.

1

1 **"APOTHEOSIS"**, Tacoma Convention Center, Washington State, USA, 2005. Architect: Wyn Bieleska. Detail showing the juxtaposed images of "ghostly" trees (to the right) and sepia relief maps.

2 **"APOTHEOSIS"** The exterior of this 240sqm (2400sqft) façade in daylight reveals nothing of the images on the glass.

2

3 **"APOTHEOSIS"** Inside the building, as the viewer looks down the staircase from above, the appearance of the glass changes completely, acting only as a mild filter between the interior and exterior.

4 **"APOTHEOSIS"** As the viewer looks upward, with the sky behind the glass, the images emerge as participants with the vertical elements of the architecture, adding another dimension to the building.

1

This glass commission at the new concourse in Seattle Tacoma Airport is well over 100m (330ft) long. The tall glass panels act as a screen between secure and non-secure areas of the airport, enclosing the route that all international travellers must pass through.

The designs, by Washington-based artist Linda Beaumont, reflect the history and the natural wonders of this Pacific Northwest landscape. Beaumont has created her photo-collage using photographs from the early 1900s, showing trees, growth rings, and loggers at work. The combination of these images into both figurative and abstract narratives evokes a powerful sense both of the ancient (some of the trees are over 1,000 years old) and of the recent history of the area.

The work has been produced using sandblasting and enamels that have been painted, airbrushed, and printed on both layers of glass prior to lamination. Unusually for a work of this scale, the artist has also used "silver stain" to achieve the rich warm glows that seem to come from

2

1 **SEA-TAC AIRPORT**,
Seattle, Washington State,
USA, 2004, 115 x 3m (380 x 10ft),
enamelled laminated glass.
A core sample of a sequoia tree,
duplicated many times, creates
a flowing image, as of wings.

2 **SEA-TAC AIRPORT**
The majestic trees of
the old-growth forest are held
in an abstract composition of
light and glass as a reminder
of their awe-inspiring power.

within the glass. Silver stain is a metal oxide that has been used in stained glass since the late 13th century. When fired at the correct temperatures it produces a range of colours from pale lemons to rich golden yellows and on to dark murky ambers. The way the oxide blends with the glass itself is different from vitreous enamels. The limitation in contemporary large works is that it does not respond well to the high temperatures used in toughening glass. Here the glass has been laminated, thus it has been fired at temperatures suitable for this "stain".

For Linda Beaumont, an experienced and versatile artist, this project was her first real experience of working with glass. It was a new discovery to be working with the added dimensions of transparency and light. She is now, in her own words, hooked on the medium, which offers so much more than two-dimensional work.

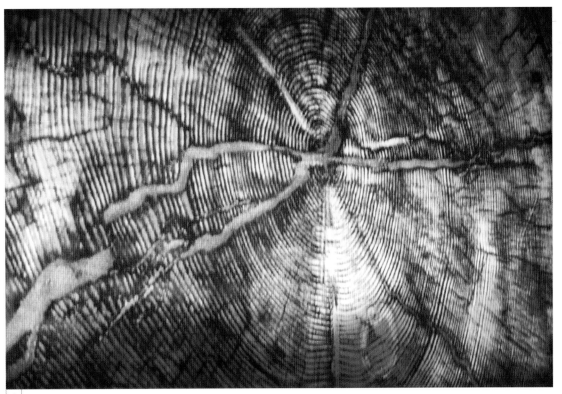

3 **SEA-TAC AIRPORT**
This picture conveys something of the scale of these panels, with their enormous images of cut tree trunks and their rich ring patterns.

4 **SEA-TAC AIRPORT**
Close up we see the way the glass appears to burn from the inside, particularly when, as here, it is animated by daylight from the exterior.

Michael Lönne and Jörn Neumann are a pair of German glass artists who have been working as a team for nearly a decade, building up a reputation for their restrained but intense designs. The glass feature shown here, located in a hospital in north-west Germany, has been entirely painted with airbrushed enamels. Each of the nine panels has been fired at least once, some up to three times. The text has been sandblasted out of the coloured glass surface after the enamel has been fired. All the panels have been made into double-glazed units, and in some areas the front of the panels has been sandblasted, partly to add more depth to the overall effect and also to reduce reflection off the front surface.

This glass feature is located in an old part of the hospital that has no natural daylight. The purpose of the back-lit project is to alleviate the absence of any existing glazing, and, at the same time, to create a friendly and welcoming space for the hospital waiting area. With this in mind the artists have used warm, soft colours with gentle gradations of colour. By designing the frames as if they were sliding glass panels, they have made it easy to change the light bulbs behind, and also intensified the sensation of the wall being merely a partition to somewhere else.

Lönne & Neumann produce a wide range of work with a distinctive flavour. They often use few but beautifully chosen and strongly contrasting colours, which create the impression of very colourful windows while in fact being made up of relatively few shades. Like many artists working in glass, much of their work is with leaded glass; however, their style shifts significantly when they work with float glass, as shown in the project featured – becoming slightly less dense, simpler, and more austere.

1

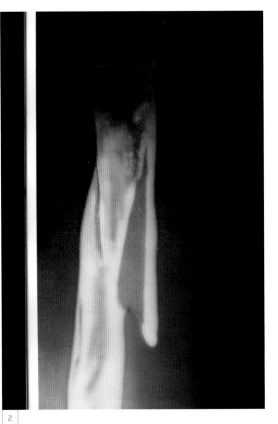

2

3

1 **ST VINCENZ HOSPITAL**, Paderborn, Germany, 2004, 10 x 2.5m (35 x 8ft). The back-lit glass feature, located in a part of the hospital with no natural daylight, has been made with airbrushed enamels on glass and sandblasted lettering.

2 **ST VINCENZ HOSPITAL** Detail from a back-lit screen showing an X-ray of a broken bone expressed in blue, which contrasts with the warm coloured background.

3 **ST VINCENZ HOSPITAL** Detail from a back-lit screen showing an X-ray of a flower, an extract of which is used in treating heart disease.

Amber Hiscott originally studied stained glass at the well-known Swansea Institute in South Wales. Since then Wales has been her home and very much part of her identity as an artist, perhaps encouraged by her natural Celtic appearance. Hiscott has earned a strong reputation as a practitioner of public art. She has completed many commissions, of which a number have been in hospitals and in other large-scale public buildings, such as the recently completed Millennium Centre in the Welsh capital, Cardiff.

Hiscott's works in glass often reflect her parallel career as a painter, translating fairly small-scale designs into large and impressive glass features. In the particular works illustrated here we see her bold sense of colour.

The 12-m (40-ft) high wall-mounted feature that dominates the entrance foyer of the brand-new Great Western Hospital (*see* below and opposite) illustrates how enamels on glass, if properly executed, can work without the need for back-lighting. Although the work

is printed in only a few colours, the final result appears fantastically rich in colour and dynamic form.

The project at the North Wales Cancer Treatment Centre demonstrates a wonderful use of glass (*see* opposite). The colourful balustrades transform the inner courtyard space as well as the surrounding balconies. The glass for these balcony walkways has been made using opaque enamels, with different areas left clear, thereby creating windows allowing views from both sides. This ensures a degree of privacy for those above, and also allows the colour to be stronger from all viewpoints. In summer, sunshine bounces off the building's corrugated metal roof, creating quirky lines in the yellow panels. Unlike transparent enamels, opaque enamels do not create the coloured "reflections" on floors and walls that we associate with traditional stained glass, hence the actual shadows that are created by light falling on the glass. The designs for these panels were evolved during workshops with children.

1

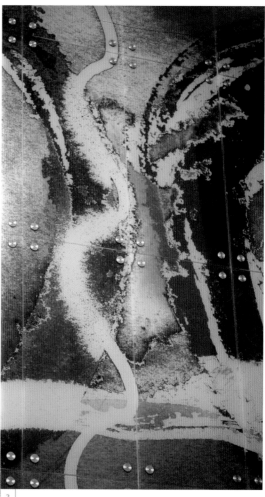

2

3

1 **"THE JOURNEY"**,
Great Western Hospital,
Swindon, England, 2002.
Wall-mounted screen in 20
panels, 4 x 10m (13 x 33ft),
opaque enamels on etch ground.

2 **"THE JOURNEY"**
Detail showing how
original watercolour design
has been expressed in screen-
printed enamels on drilled,
toughened float glass. No
back-lighting is required.

3 **NORTH WALES CANCER
TREATMENT CENTRE**,
Glan Clwyd Hospital, Wales, 2001.
25 panels, each approximately
1 x 2m (3 x 6.5ft), creating
tall, enclosing balcony
screens, here viewed from
the landscaped garden below.

4 **NORTH WALES CANCER
TREATMENT CENTRE**
The screens as viewed from
the balconies, showing the
multi-coloured designs evolved in
collaboration with local children,
with transparent areas allowing
vision through to the courtyard.

4

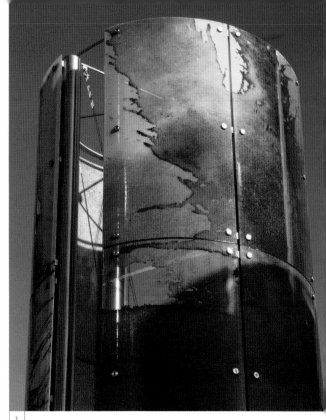

1

British artist David Pearl has worked as a glass artist in the UK and Canada for 25 years. He is a designer who does not have a style, as such, more a way of thinking and working and a desire to do different things, conceptually, structurally, and technically. It very much illustrates Pearl's inquisitive approach to his art that he recently completed a Master's degree at London's prestigious Bartlett College of Architecture, challenging himself to learn new skills and new ways of thinking, and working beside students up to 20 years younger than himself. He is now adding photography and video to his repertoire of skills.

The Cardiff "Water Towers" project (*see* right) required all of Pearl's skills and commitment to detail

1 **"WATER TOWERS"**, Cardiff, Wales, 2000. Each tower is 5m (16ft) in circumference and 10m (33ft) tall and made of 16 panels of toughened, laminated, curved glass, each panel measuring 1.25 x 2.5m (4 x 8ft). The image is taken from a watercolour by Amber Hiscott.

2

2 **PRINCESS OF WALES HOSPITAL**, Bridgend, Wales, 1999. Interior curved screen 7 x 2.1m (23 x 7ft). Opaque and transparent enamels on curved laminated glass.

3 **BASINGSTOKE LIDO**, Basingstoke, England, 2002, 4 x 6m (13 x 20ft). One of seven windows made for this competition pool. The image is based on photographic studies of light on water.

3

4

5

to bring it to fruition. Pearl went through several installation proposals, refining the structure until the glass became the major feature rather than the adjunct to a steel structure, as first envisaged. The tower illustrates how opaque enamels work in both transmitted and reflected light, the work performing as well in the daylight as at night.

The curved screen, shown opposite, is a mixture of opaque and transparent colours. The opaque blue helps visually to retain the curving form of the glass, and the clear horizontal lines help to articulate the undulating curves of the screen. The image of a reclining figure, expressed as transparent pink and yellow, is set against the blue background. The result is a dividing structure that allows some visual penetration, and has that brilliant shine that comes from small transparent apertures in an opaque surface. The screen is supported at the floor and ceiling by elegant minimalist stainless-steel plates.

4 **"WATER TOWERS"**
The sculpture is set in a circular pool of water. Fountains are set behind the glass, so that the towers appear as illuminated columns of colour emerging from the mists of the floodlit water.

5 **"WATER TOWERS"**
The towers are seen here illuminated by sunlight. They are supported by stainless-steel columns that are engineered to withstand tremendous wind pressures by an internally tensioned cable system.

TOBIAS KAMMERER

Tobias Kammerer is from southern Germany and studied painting and sculpture in Vienna in the late 1980s. As for many glass artists, his discovery of glass as a medium was a moment of illumination. Kammerer creates models to explore how an image will respond to different types of light. He is clearly part of the tradition of painter/glass artist, his works resembling very large paintings executed in glass, with all the beauty of the grand brushstroke and the modulations of tone and depth as colours traverse over one another. Kammerer has a distinctive style that works just as well in churches as in secular contexts. Very experienced in glass, he does much of the work of interpretation himself, working with a professional glass studio. With both of the works shown here we see his interest in the interplay of translucence and transparency.

The drama of his five-storey staircase for a steel company illustrates how successful it can be to exploit these wonderful contexts with the use of colour on glass. Staircases often get a great deal of use, yet at the same time they are merely spaces for passing through: nobody actually works or concentrates there. As such, they provide a perfect opportunity for dramatic statements in glass. The external appearance, particularly at night, can become a major feature of the landscape and, as in this case, a signature for the company that commissioned the work.

Kammerer's 23-m (75-ft) long screen for the Volksbank in Nagold (*see* pp.94–5) is a good example of his mature work. The design feels simple: its component pieces are interacting rather than overlapping; the colours are straightforward, strong and contrasting; the forms are very clearly defined. Although in this image we see only a part of the overall screen, the complete effect is a balance of drama and repose, of intensity and calm.

1

2

3

3

1 **HAGENER FEINSTAHL**, Hagen, Germany, 1998. Exterior view of the stairwell artwork that has created a major landmark at a large intersection.

2 **HAGENER FEINSTAHL** This detail shows how intense the colours can be, and the way in which transparent and translucent glass interacts, giving totally different perspectives.

3 **HAGENER FEINSTAHL** Stairwells offer some of the best opportunities for glass art. Often much used by occupants, they are spaces of transience that benefit from added drama.

4 (Overleaf) **VOLKSBANK**, Nagold, Germany, 2001. This wave-like, semi-transparent partition wall transforms the spaces on both sides. The glass can be partly folded for changes of use.

Sasha Ward's route to becoming a glass artist is unusual. She spent three years studying the making of stained-glass windows, followed by three years at art college, and finally completed a two-year postgraduate course at the highly selective Royal College of Art in London. This route is the reverse of the creative journeys of many glass artists, who often "end up" in glass after trying many other different media.

From the start of her professional career Ward has been interested in painting with enamels onto float glass. Most of her projects have been made in collaboration with a large studio, but she makes all the initial samples herself in her own studio. Recently she has expanded her own equipment to enable her to do more of the actual manufacture of the glass.

The swimming pool project illustrated here is very architectural in concept and execution. The main panels are quite graphic in conception, while the detail image (right) shows how the simple concept became more complex as it was evolved in other areas of the building.

The 13-m (43-ft) tall hanging feature shown opposite was an ambitious work in every sense. The design, as seen

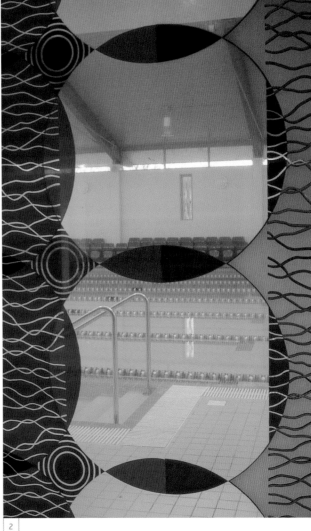

2

from below, is relatively simple and bold, contrasting an apparently opaque orange shape with a transparent blue shape. But as we see in the detail picture, once viewed up close from inside the elevator car the panels are revealed to be full of roughly drawn details.

Ward's work is very much a balance of clinical shapes and forms and quite roughly expressed organic details. She is a master of enamel colours and uses a broad palette, all derived from her own detailed experiments with mixing and firing enamels onto glass.

1

1 **CARTERTON LEISURE CENTRE**, near Oxford, England, 2003. Architect: Childs & Sulzmann. Printed in three different blues, the design on the window becomes integrated into the architecture.

2 **CARTERTON LEISURE CENTRE** A detail from one of two internal panels, each 1.5 x 2.4m (5 x 8ft), that elaborate on the theme.

3

3 **"INTREPID STEPS"**,
Principality Building
Society, Cardiff, Wales, 1992,
1 x 13m (3 x 43ft). This
ambitious hanging commission
has a strong form when
viewed from below.

4 **"INTREPID STEPS"**
This view from the
passing elevator shows the
very intricate details that
are visible from up close.

4

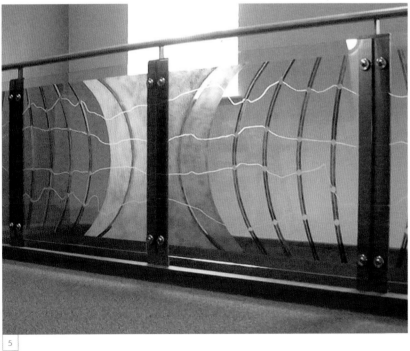

5

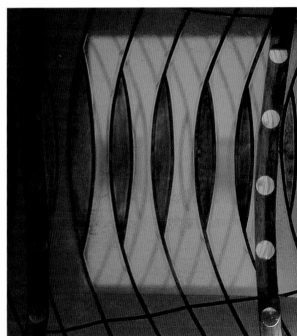

6

5 **COTSWOLD DISTRICT
COUNTY OFFICES**,
Cirencester, England, 2002.
These beautiful balustrades
introduce a curvilinear
form to typically rectangular
balustrade panels.

6 **THE CHAPLAINCY**,
Great Western Hospital ,
Swindon, England, 2002. This
detail shows how Ward has
worked with two layers of
glass – the patterns mingling
to create additional images.

Udo Zembok has been an architectural glass artist for 30 years. He has never worked in stained glass, working at first with laminated antique glass, and now mainly with enamels and multilayered fused float glass with pigment and mineral inclusions, using additional techniques such as slumping or bending. He experiments with smaller art objects – thick glass "sculptural" pieces that he exhibits in art galleries – using these to help develop the ideas and techniques he brings to his larger architectural work.

In this simulation of a series of nine windows for a Swiss Presbyterian church, we see a highly innovative work in development. Some of the panels will be 3.2m (10 ft) high and 1.2 m (4 ft) wide, each made from two layers of low-iron "crystal" glass, with inclusions of enamels, sprayed and painted onto the glass prior to fusing the two layers in the kiln. These large-scale windows are being manufactured with the help of a glass studio in Strasbourg, France.

In his work for a bank's offices in the north-east of France, Zembok has made a series of relatively simple panels for the main office partitioning. In front of these he has created a single free-standing work. It is the wonderful movements in the colours that he has created that are at the centre of this piece. This is probably characteristic of the sort of work that can only really be created by an artist in his own studio, manufacturing his own pieces. It is the result of playing with glass, developing a feeling for what colours do when they are given a little space and a little heat.

The panel for the Waldorf School is very much about enhancing the exterior view while still creating a partial barrier. The colours of the glass have been carefully blended with the colours of the exterior. Zembok is a colourist with a refined feeling for the exact amount of delicate touch needed to accomplish a great work.

1 **16TH-CENTURY PRESBYTERIAN CHURCH**, Geneva, Switzerland, 2005, nine windows, each 1.2 x 3.2m (4 x 10ft). Double layer of fused float glass with inclusions of coloured frit and surface enamelling. Enamels are airbrushed onto the glass.

1

2

2 **CREDIT MUTUEL BANK**, Colmar, France, 2003, 2.6 x 4.5m (8.5 x 15ft). Internal separation wall with a single art panel of slumped and airbrushed enamel on float glass.

3

3 **WALDORF SCHOOL**,
Frankenthal, Germany,
2002, 1.45 x 3.6m (5 x 12ft).
A decorative panel of slumped
and airbrushed enamels
on float glass.

Saskia Schultz is a young German artist, and her work is very much about using bands of colour to create moods and atmosphere, and then adding texture to the colour through the use of some form of irregular organic pattern – in the project shown here, a net motif.

This glass feature was commissioned for the chapel of a detoxification centre in Wilhelmsdorf, Germany. The purpose was to create some privacy in a space that is designed for prayer or meditation, and for occasional church services. The vertical coloured panels are a way of creating a soft but containing screen that prevents people from looking in, but enables those inside to view out. The artist has used the imagery of nets to add a texture and a second colour to some of the panels.

Each panel has been printed with a single colour and then fired. The net structure has then been sandblasted away to some depth. The net shape has subsequently been filled with a second enamel colour and the glass refired. Finally, in some panels, words have been added, sandblasted out of the base colour.

The panels are designed so that they can be slid along the track to create different configurations. Although the panels appear relatively transparent, they create a very private space inside the building. But it is the choice of the soft, contrasting pastel colours that allows the space to be bathed in a serene and peaceful light.

The combination of enamelling the glass and then removing parts by sandblasting or acid-etching offers the perfect expression for Schultz' vision. Here, because of the simplicity of the style, the work blends well into this very contemporary, seamless, frameless environment, where there is no explicit canvas to work to, and where the brief is not to shut out the entire wall, but simply to interrupt it.

1

2

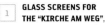

1 **GLASS SCREENS FOR THE "KIRCHE AM WEG"**, Wilhelmsdorf, Germany, 2004. Architect: Single & Weinbrenner. The screens frame the chapel in this detoxification and rehabilitation centre.

2 **"KIRCHE AM WEG"** The glass has been printed all over in one colour; the detailed net pattern has been sandblasted away up to 1.5mm (0.1in) deep. This relief has been filled with enamel and the panels refired.

3 **"KIRCHE AM WEG"** The tall panels, fitting into slots top and bottom, form adjustable secondary glazing that creates privacy in some parts of the space, as well as transforming a cool interior.

1 **AL FAISALIAH CENTRE**, Riyadh, Saudi Arabia, 1999, 2,000sqm (21,500sqft). Architect: Norman Foster. From a distance the image, printed with large well-spaced dots, appears like a vast photograph on glass, but as the viewer gets nearer it fragments into increasingly abstract compositions made up of beautifully interweaving colours.

2 **AL FAISALIAH CENTRE** Clarke worked closely with the architect to design this stained-glass window, the largest in the world, which vibrates with shimmering colours. Images of the desert and classic figurative icons from Saudi Arabia form a vast visual panorama.

Twenty-five years ago Brian Clarke was one of a tiny handful of stained-glass artists who were committed to transforming this medium and to bringing it into the secular arena. It is hard to remember now how completely everyone assumed that stained glass belonged in churches. Clarke learned all he could from four or five legendary German post-war artists, brought back his vision to the UK, and converted this previously ecclesiastical medium into a language available for contemporary secular buildings. In the 1980s and '90s Clarke created many projects in various countries that were more than 1,000sqm (10,800sqft) in scale, and that all used leaded glass.

Although Clarke had used screen-printed images in his stained-glass work as early as 1981, it was not until the late 1990s that he began to explore fully the potential of working with enamels and float glass. Since then he has designed a number of large schemes, of

3

which the largest – and also his first completely screen-printed work – is shown on p.102. For the entrance façade of this skyscraper in Saudi Arabia Clarke worked closely with the architect Norman Foster to achieve a number of different objectives, including reducing the solar gain that would otherwise have been enormous. The work is filled with images that reflect the culture, topography, and history of the location, which makes it an unusual work in a part of the world where figurative art is rare.

Meanwhile, as the examples on these pages show, Clarke continues to press those in a position to convert visions into reality, to have the imagination to see how incorporating colour and contour into the glazing of buildings can add so much to the external cityscape, as well as to the experience of those within the building.

4

3 **ASCOT GRANDSTAND**,
Berkshire, England, 2007.
Architect: HOK Sport. Will this grand scheme be incorporated into the final construction? In real life the work will feel like a shimmering veil over the façade.

4 **ASCOT GRANDSTAND**
As seen from the interior.
The work is to be executed with transparent enamels, so that viewers will still be able to see out through the glass, as if through a screen of leaves.

5

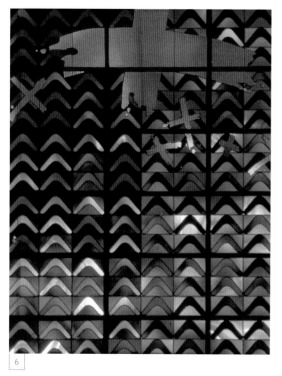

6

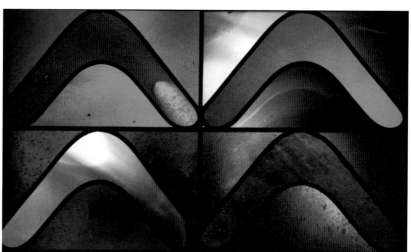

7

5   **GLASS DUNE**, Ministry of the Environment Building, Hamburg, Germany, 1994. Architect: Future Systems. This proposed building incorporates a huge area of coloured, leaded glass.

6   **GLASS DUNE** The full-size sample of leaded glass shows Clarke's sense of merging art and architecture; simple repeated shapes that echo the building, invaded with occasional disruptive forms.

7   **GLASS DUNE** Detail of sample. Would Clarke do this as leaded glass today? Would the beauty of the mouth-blown glass outweigh all the advantages and savings of producing the work in enamels?

8

9

8 **PROPOSAL FOR NORTH FAÇADE, WEST WINTER GARDEN**, Heron Quays, Canary Wharf, London, England, 2001. Architect: Cesar Pelli & Associates. This proposal was never accepted, which is a tragedy. The cost would not have been huge, and perhaps repeated images could have been used without anybody knowing.

9 **PROPOSAL FOR NORTH FAÇADE, WEST WINTER GARDEN** Because enamels, even transparent enamels, are more reflective than mouth-blown glass, this building would have looked as fantastic from the inside as from outside.

Graham Jones has been a powerful influence as a glass artist for a number of years. Many artists relate that when they saw what Jones could achieve with glass it opened their eyes to whole new areas of potential. During the 1980s and early '90s he worked exclusively with leaded glass, but over the past decade more and more of his work has been realized using enamelled colours on large panes of float glass.

As a stained-glass artist Jones always had a very liberated approach to the medium, using the techniques of acid-etching and painting but always trying to create a loose, spontaneous, and dynamic relationship with these crafts – more like a Jackson Pollock than a Mondrian.

Being a painter, and himself a superb craftsman in glass, Jones was at first sceptical of the capacity of enamels on float glass to do justice to his glass art. However, over time he realized he could use the technique to convert the flat, inanimate surface of float glass into something alive and dynamic. The colours he was painting in, although printed, could capture the energy of his original brushstroke. Having always revelled in the texture and uniqueness of every piece of mouth-blown glass, Jones found he could create texture in the float glass. The major difference is that now he is more likely to be putting on the resists for the acid with a broom than with a small paintbrush. The scale is different but the effect is the same.

As these images show, Jones is primarily a painter who works in glass, converting his canvases into large expressionist works of art. He is a wonderful colourist, actively seeking to create some form of dynamic tension in his works, otherwise they will "lack any real life". Now based in south-west England, he has made works for sites on almost every continent and in every imaginable context, but particularly churches and corporate headquarters.

1

1 **BRITISH GAS CONFERENCE ROOM**, Reading, England, 2002. Glass screen c. 9 x 2.7m (30 x 9ft), viewed from the interior. Screen-printed in transparent and opaque enamels in several colours.

2 **BRITISH GAS CONFERENCE ROOM** The exterior corridor image of the long screen shows Jones' typical use of acid-etching and sandblasting to animate the surface of the glass.

3

4

5

3 BAT, Corporate Headquarters, London, England, 2001. The food area of this office canteen has back-lit panels with characteristic broad brushstrokes in red and black, and bonded elements on the surface.

4 BAT The main eating area of the canteen is decorated with blue brushstrokes. The panels hang from the ceiling on sliding rails, with low-voltage lights at top and bottom.

5 BAT This detail shows the slumped-glass rectangular shapes that add geometric forms to the overall composition and also give texture and luminescence to the surface of the glass.

6

7

8

6 **HOLMES PLACE HEALTH CLUB, KENSINGTON**,
London, England, 1999, 7 x 7m (23 x 23ft). This planar wall is made of laminated glass, with stainless-steel fixings. Enamel colours are screen-printed on the inside face.

7 **HOLMES PLACE HEALTH CLUB, KENSINGTON**
The same wall, viewed from the other side. This shows how differently the same work can appear, depending on diverse factors such as the time of day and lighting conditions.

8 **HOLMES PLACE HEALTH CLUB, KENSINGTON**
This picture, taken from the stairs looking down, shows how the glass appears up close: it contains the space, but allows some visibility through to the other side.

9

9 **HOLMES PLACE HEALTH CLUB, LISBON,** Portugal, 2001. This shows the top half of a glass wall that extends over two floors. Some areas were left transparent specifically to enable visibility through to the pool.

10 **HOLMES PLACE HEALTH CLUB, LISBON** This photograph shows the view from the poolside, with the coloured image reflecting in the water, and revealing a partial view into the interior.

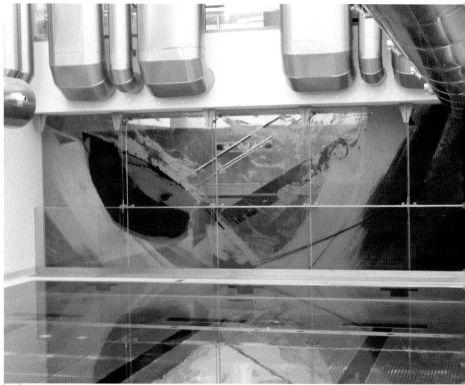

11

11 **BRITISH TELECOM INTERNATIONAL HEADQUARTERS**, Oswestry, Wales, 2001. This dynamic, energy-filled screen is adjacent to the reception desk for this corporate HQ. We see again the characteristic splashed acid-etched texture to the glass, animating the "canvas".

12 **CENTRICA CORPORATE HEADQUARTERS**, Windsor, England, 2004. Fired enamel colours can be forgiving of lighting, unlike stained glass. This "front-lit", wall-mounted panel shows how well enamels can be made to reflect light.

Alexander Beleschenko has been one of the foremost glass artists working in the UK since the early 1980s. He was a pioneer in the early experiments to move away from the use of leaded antique glass. His initial works used a technique of sandwiching antique glass between two layers of float glass. This had merits but also its drawbacks: the panels tended to be heavy, they were exacting to execute, and the front pane of float glass tended to act as a mirror, obscuring the work behind.

Beleschenko has always experimented in his own studio, using fragments of glass and different pigments, resins, treatments, and methods. He explores all the processes that are used industrially to see if they can also be used artistically, and keeps coming up with new ideas, new ways of playing with the medium.

Many architectural glass artists will say that their designs are site-specific, yet Beleschenko is one of those of whom this is unusually true. He has no obvious style,

and it would be difficult to spot his work unless one knew he was the author. Each project seems to bring out some relatively new idea, technique, or approach, which might be subsequently discarded as he moves on.

The projects on these pages show Beleschenko working in collaboration with an architectural practice, using his skills and vision to add dimension to a concept. The vast doors of the church, opposite, show his understanding of how architecture works. This is not a painting in glass: it is a texture and a colour when seen from afar, but emerges into imagery and detail as the viewer approaches. In the Canary Wharf pedestrian link (*see* pp.114–15) he does something that plays with repetition but is somehow full of incident in the particular.

Beleschenko's projects have sometimes been controversial because he takes great risks, inventing and reinventing himself and the medium within which he works. But his creations are always exciting as architectural art.

1 **MILLENNIUM BRIDGE**, Coventry, England, 2003. Architect: MJP Architects. A total of 798 curved glass "fins" form the balustrade of this new bridge and transform the steel structure into a delicate twisting flourish of colour and light.

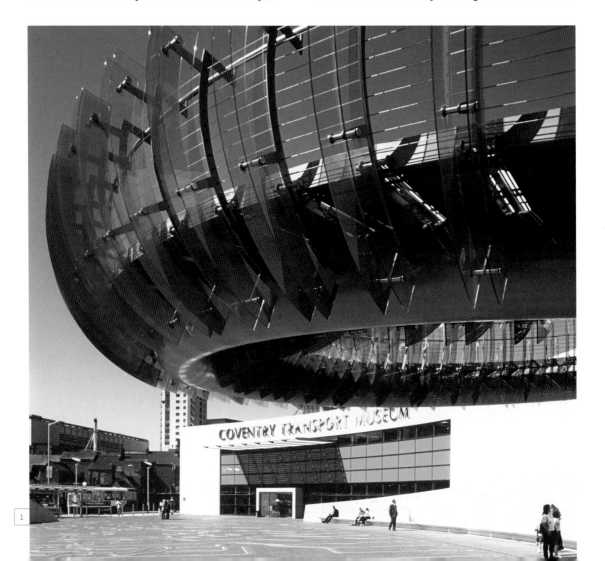

2

HERZ JESUS KIRCHE,
Munich, Germany, 2001,
225sqm (2,400sqft). Architect:
Allmann, Sattler, Wappner.
Two 14-m (45-ft) high opening
doors are each made up of 432
enamelled double-glazed panels
with printing on more than
one layer of glass.

HERZ JESUS KIRCHE
Images of nails are used
cryptographically to create a text
and a texture on the glass.

HERZ JESUS KIRCHE
This dramatic view shows
the vast doors, supported on
internal wheels, rolled open like
two welcoming arms.

3

4

6

7

5 **CANARY WHARF
PEDESTRIAN LINK**,
London, England, 2001. Architect:
Cesar Pelli & Associates. Three
back-lit glass walls, totalling
120sqm (1,290sqft). Each panel
measures 1.2 x 1.4m (3.9 x 4.6ft).

6 **CANARY WHARF
PEDESTRIAN LINK**
The architectural regularity is
in contradiction to the basic
shape, the constantly shifting
colours, and the occasional
irregularities and gaps.

7 **CANARY WHARF
PEDESTRIAN LINK**
The walls are made up of
hundreds of coloured shapes,
creating waves of dancing
colour across the wall.

Stuart Reid is an artist/architect living and working in Toronto, Canada. Among many other distinctions he is a professor of design at the Ontario College of Art and Design. He has been working as a glass artist for many years, most of that time in the traditional mode of stained-glass artist. Yet the three recent commissions shown here reveal how, for some artists, moving away from the use of lead can act as a total liberation. It is as if the artist is suddenly put in touch with a whole new dimension of his or her creative being, one that has perhaps been present all along, but has not properly found expression through the medium of glass.

Reid's 21st-century output has been joyful, liberated, and more profoundly connected with the language and issues that confront architecture and the construction processes of the modern urban environment.

Looking at Reid's hotel reception desk feature we see a brilliant glass screen that excites the imagination, but also enhances the pure clean lines of the architecture. He has used a fairly confined palette but introduced many different gradations of tone, creating the sense of many colours vibrating with each other. The contrasting blues and ambers are very dynamic, but the strongly expressed

geometric elements give the piece a sense of structure and cohesion. The whole expresses a combination of luxurious relaxation and calm, together with the intense energies of a dynamic urban environment.

The client liked the reception feature so much that he commissioned a parallel piece for the restaurant/bar (see p.118). Again Reid works with simple geometric vertical lines and rectangular forms, but within this he plays with subtle tonal gradations.

"Homage to Mozart" is located in the Salzburg Congress building, a brand new conference centre in Salzburg, Austria. Here Reid's work is a classic example of a sensual element acting to add essential seasoning to the rationalism of the architecture. In the same way that art galleries are often purist white boxes whose minimalism enhances the beauty of the artworks, so a pure piece of architectural art can breathe life into the empty matrix of a contemporary interior space.

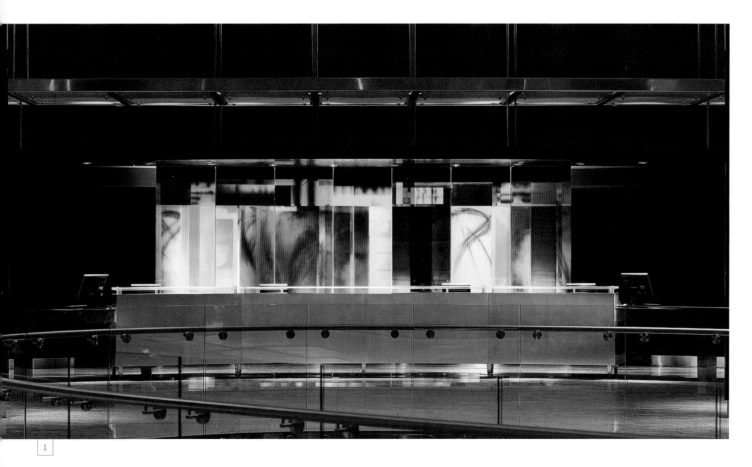

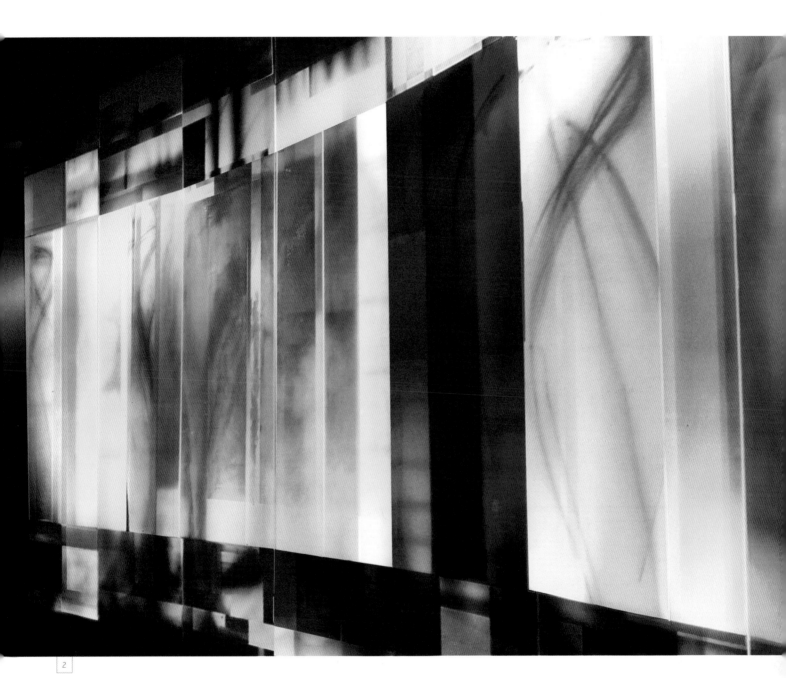

2

1 **"URBAN RIBBON"**,
InterContinental Toronto
Centre Hotel, Toronto, Canada,
2003, 6 x 3m (20 x 10ft). A
curved, back-lit feature behind
the reception desk, the work is
made entirely with enamels fired
onto float glass – two sheets
thick and laminated together.

2 **"URBAN RIBBON"** This
close-up of the same
work shows the way in which
the two layers of overlaid
glass create additional colours.

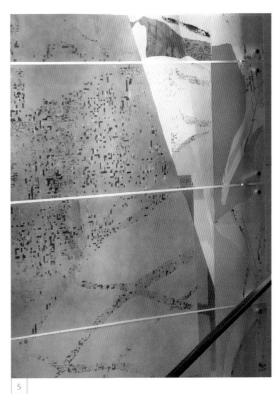

4

"LIQUID VEIL",
3   InterContinental Toronto
Centre Hotel, Toronto, Canada,
2003. Reid's second commision
for the hotel was this artwork
in the restaurant/bar.

"HOMAGE TO MOZART",
4   Salzburg Congress,
Salzburg, Austria, 2001.
Sited in a new conference centre,
the work descends through two
stories beside the escalators.

5

"HOMAGE TO MOZART"
5   The work is made up of
20 sheets of float glass, each
3 x 1m (10 x 3ft), with painted
and airbrushed enamels.

"HOMAGE TO MOZART"
6   The commission was
proposed to act specifically
as a "romantic counterpoint
to a modernist environment".

6

1   **SAGE CENTRE**, Gateshead, England, 2004. Architect: Foster & Partners. This picture shows the way the enamelled curved glass balustrades emphasize the rippling structure of the building.

2   **SAGE CENTRE** The colours are deep transparent enamels fired into the glass, executed with the precision that minimalism always demands.

2

Kate Maestri's work is in the tradition of Josef Albers and those who have followed on afterward in the exploration of interactive colours – eschewing texture, narrative content, and expressive allusions. Because of this purity of intent and focus, Maestri's work has a natural appeal to the architectural purist. Her work does not introduce competing rhythms, dynamics, or forms into a space, but, as can be seen in these images, the simplicity of the design helps to elucidate and emphasize the shapes and forms already created by the building. In this sense Maestri is a classic "architect's artist".

Maestri was the almost inevitable winner of a shortlisted competition to find an artist to work with Foster & Partners in designing the 100-m (330-ft) long glass balustrade at Tyneside's spectacular new live-music centre, The Sage Gateshead. Her designs, like most works of a minimalist nature, require a certain confidence on the part of the practitioner, as so little seems to be happening. The ideas seem so simple, yet the result can be surprisingly potent. For the glass fabricators the technical demands of this sort of design, where the glass is void of detail and texture and hence there is nothing to hide the slightest blemish in the colours, are extreme.

The glass canopy in London's Hanover Square (*see* p.122) illustrates well a classic context in which enamelled glass can easily be used. It adds an extra element to the public space outside, to the identity and façade of the building itself, and to the experience of entering and leaving the building.

Finally, in the back-lit panel for a private house (*see* p.123), we see a classic example of Maestri's work in a domestic context. Unlike many architectural glass artists, Maestri exhibits at galleries quite regularly, and sells autonomous works that can easily be wall-mounted and are already being collected by a discerning few.

3

4

3 4 **SAGE CENTRE**
These images illustrate how the design strengthens and helps to articulate the architecture, without being subservient or merely ornamental.

7

5 **HANOVER STREET**, London, England, 2000, 4 x 1.5m (13 x 5ft). A transparent glass canopy, executed in toughened enamelled glass, is laminated for safety.

6 **VAUXHALL BRIDGE ROAD**, London, England, 2004, 13 x 1.8m (43 x 6ft). A translucent glass canopy in toughened laminated enamelled glass. The warm colours are visible from a distance, making a feature of this entranceway.

5

6

7 **ST JAMES'S STREET**, London, England, 2001, 8 x 2.4m (26 x 8ft). An office reception feature in curved glass panels: the work is lit only with downlighters, but the enamels hold their colour perfectly.

8 **PRIVATE RESIDENCE**, 2004, 2.5 x 6m (8 x 20ft). A classic Kate Maestri work: a study in warm colours, located behind a kitchen sink in a private residence, and artificially lit.

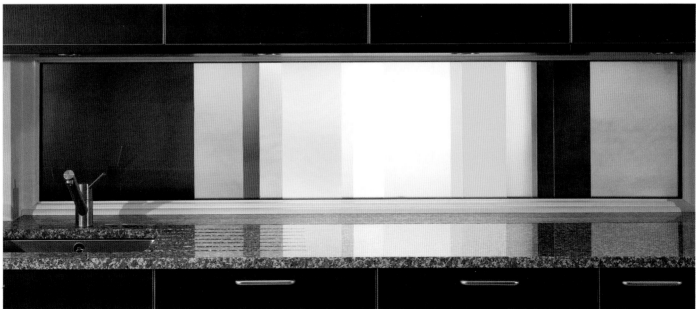

8

The term "lamination" is used here to refer to any process of bonding together different layers of glass. This might include: UV-bonding bevelled glass pieces onto float glass; bonding mouth-blown glass to float glass; laminating dichroic glass; or working on the interlayer between two layers of glass.

For many glass artists, the unique material that is mouth-blown glass – often referred to as "antique" glass – is central to the process of creating architectural glass art. Mouth-blown glass is still made as it was more than 1,000 years ago, by blowing up a large tubelike bottle, cutting off the two ends, and opening up the cylinder, thus creating a flat sheet. Mouth-blown glass comes in a vast range of colours and in many different textures. It can come as transparent or translucent, or it can come as a thin layer of colour on a clear or opalescent base, which can then

be etched away creating beautiful gradations of colour. Many of those involved in stained glass become so enraptured by the first piece of antique glass they pick up that they devote their life to working with this jewel-like medium on the strength of the experience.

The process of bonding antique glass to float glass is more time-consuming than leading and soldering. Every piece of glass must be polished to ensure the edges join perfectly. If the shapes are complicated, the pieces have to be ground into perfectly matching profiles.

The benefit of laminating antique glass to float glass, rather than binding the pieces together with a latticework of lead, is that all the beauty of the colours is retained. Large glass panels can be assembled to create seamless, frameless walls of glass that integrate into the vocabulary of modern buildings.

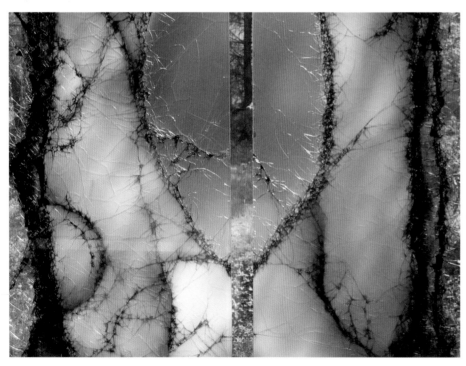

ABOVE **LAMINATED PANELS**, private residence, London, England, 2004: by Yorgos Papadopolous. The panels are pictured before installation, in a back-lit context, standing against a background of green grass. Sunlight strikes the fractured edges, revealing the dynamic potential of this technique.

TOP **MCGRAW HILL RECEPTION**, Canary Wharf, London, England, 2004: by Kate Maestri. A deceptively simple back-lit laminated feature, this work exploits the innate beauty of mouth-blown glass, and the subtle colours and unique modulations within each piece of glass.

ABOVE **INTERIOR PANEL**, private residence, London, England, 2003: by Stuart Low. This beautifully etched panel is brought to life by numerous polished antique glass pieces bonded to the surface.

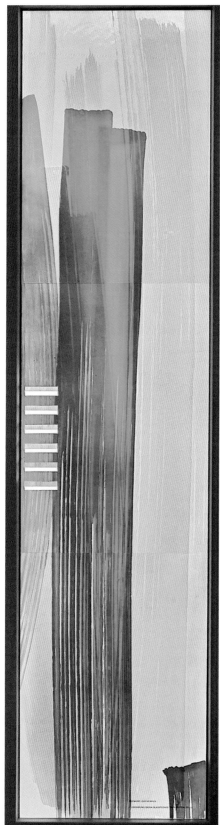

ABOVE & RIGHT **"INTO THE SUN"**, panel for a cemetery chapel, Engenhahn, Germany, 2005, 64 x 240cm (25 x 95ft): by Guy Kemper. The panel is made from mouth-blown glass, laminated in two layers to float glass. One layer is etched flashed green antique, with a plated layer of silver-stained opal. The bevels are laminated onto the float background. The subtle gradations of yellows and greens are shown in the detail (above).

Bert Glauner grew up and studied in post-war Germany, but emigrated to Mexico in the early 1960s. For 20 years he worked as a jewellery designer for several large companies. His discovery of glass came during the 1980s, at an age when some people would have been contemplating retirement. At that time contemporary architectural glass art was almost completely unknown in Mexico, and Glauner has been a major player in helping to create awareness of this new medium. His studio is a base for international glass celebrities to hold workshops and seminars, and he encouraged galleries and museums to hold exhibitions.

"Kubos" (below) is a typically original work by Glauner. The piece is installed in the entrance lobby of a large apartment. The free-standing monolithic wall of cream-coloured, acid-etched marble is penetrated by four glass forms, so that on each side four cube shapes appear. The outer surface of these is sandblasted. Inside there are small sculptures made of coloured glass pieces. When the central lights are turned on, distorted images of the sculptures are projected onto the outer skin. Because the images are projected they move as the viewer moves. The overall experience is intriguing: there is a mysterious feeling, as the shapes are never clearly defined and their source is not easily located.

The apartment screen and the exterior terrace screen shown opposite are typical of Glauner's work. The make-up of the glass involves a basic structural glass, in both cases a laminated glass, with sandblasting creating areas of translucence and areas of transparency. Coloured and different-textured glasses are bonded on, including bevelled glass, kiln-formed glass, and industrial reeded glass. In the case of the exterior terrace screen it is this building up of layers that makes the composition so dynamic, because sunlight plays with the glass, making its images dance on the floor and change throughout the day.

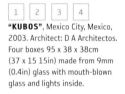

| 1 | 2 | 3 | 4 |

"KUBOS", Mexico City, Mexico, 2003. Architect: D A Architectos. Four boxes 95 x 38 x 38cm (37 x 15 15in) made from 9mm (0.4in) glass with mouth-blown glass and lights inside.

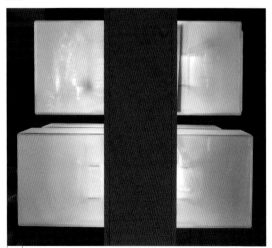

5 **OPEN AIR SCREEN**, private residence, Morelos, Mexico, 2000. This screen forms one side of a large shaded terrace. Many different types of coloured and textured glass, some with a pigmented interlayer, are laminated to the basic structural glass.

6 **INTERNAL GLASS SCREEN**, private residence, Mexico City, Mexico, 2003. Large areas of the screen are left entirely clear, thus creating the desired spatial separation while allowing a clear view through from certain angles.

5

6

Peter Kuckei is an established German artist who works with prints, oil paintings, object design, and also, since the mid-1990s, glass. Kuckei lives in Germany and the United States, and exhibits his works all over the world. Since 2002 his US residence has been in Miami, Florida. Kuckei believes the landmark public artwork, shown below, will encourage others to see the possibilities of incorporating glass art into architecture. This 125-sqm (1,345-sqft) work makes up the exterior glazing of a four-storey tall semi-circular tower, the centrepiece of a new luxury apartment building. The glass art is visible from afar, asserting the building's presence and affirming its name, "Place of Arts". This project is Kuckei's first work in a speculative residential context, and represents a bold initiative by his client.

Kuckei's relatively few projects in glass have used mostly mouth-blown glass laminated to float glass. For Kuckei the shimmering beauty of the colours and the animated texture of blown glass cannot be matched by other methods. As an oil painter, the quality and feel of the medium is all-important to him, and working with mouth-blown glass feels to him most like painting with oils. In the pictures here we can see how easy it is to retain a high degree of transparency while at the same time creating privacy. It is indicative of the sophistication of Kuckei's approach to design that he has exploited the colours in the exterior landscape to make them integral parts of the overall composition.

A work of this sort cannot be captured in a few still pictures. Each of the four windows will look entirely different depending on the time of day, the season, the weather, and the angle of vision. Nothing about this work of art will remain static – it is many different experiences and works of art captured in one commission.

1

1 **PLACE DES ARTS**, Fort Lauderdale, Florida, USA, 2005. Architect: Shane Ames. Developer: Azur International. The building is a development of luxury apartments.

2

3

4

PLACE DES ARTS

2 3 The building has four floors, each with nine panels measuring approx. 1.15 x 3m (4 x 10ft). From the interior, the colours of the outside – the greens of the palm trees and the blues of the sky – form part of the design.

PLACE DES ARTS

4 In the Florida morning sunlight the mouth-blown glass creates shimmering, changing colours on the floor. The semi-transparency of the glass reveals something of the exterior without allowing others to look in.

1

2

Dorothy Lenehan is a true artist/craftsperson who takes almost as much pleasure in the construction of her pieces as in the design. She grew up painting and drawing, but her real interest was in making things: when she began to work in glass she felt that she had finally found the perfect material. In 1983 Lenehan moved to San Francisco to work with Narcissus Quagliata (see pp.156–7), fabricating his extraordinarily challenging and detailed leaded portraits. Later, she assisted in his large fused works, developing more and more skills as a gifted glass worker. From the mid-1990s Lenehan has been running her own studio.

The screen for Pacific Bell (shown on this page) is executed on 12-mm (0.5-in) toughened low-iron glass that has been sandblasted and acid-etched on both sides, and then had cut and acid-etched pieces of mouth-blown glass bonded to its surface. The glass is worked on both sides so that the images overlay one another. The stainless-steel structural elements were designed by Dennis Luedeman. The glass "gates" for Macy's (opposite) use the same techniques, involving working on both sides of the glass, and are equally excellently engineered to achieve a complex brief with very minimal structure.

Like many glass artists who work with blown glass, Lenehan designs mainly using collages of coloured paper, folding, gluing, drawing, and painting. "I love to work with true beautiful colour. The only way I can achieve that stunning transparent colour is working with blown glass, usually flashed glass, so that I can then use acid to shade it to the perfect tones I am looking for. There is nothing like the light coming through beautiful blown glass, both the flat blown glass, or the thicker roundels that I have specially blown for me and then break up and polish and use as 'stones' in some pieces."

1 **PACIFIC BELL OFFICES**,
San Francisco, USA, 1999.
Detail from the low-iron glass screen, showing how both sides of the glass have been worked.

2 **PACIFIC BELL OFFICES**
This image shows the whole screen. It is made with a combination of sandblasting, acid-etching, and bonded blown glass.

3

4

3   **"INVISIBLE FENCES"**, Macy's Union Square, San Francisco, USA, 2000. These gates allow the store to close off some areas while allowing access to the upstairs restaurant. When opened, the glass swings through 270 degrees and becomes part of the other wall of glass.

4   **"INVISIBLE FENCES"** This detail shows the acid-etched and painted blown glass abutting the etching on the float-glass base.

Having studied glass in Swansea, Wales, Sachiko Yamamoto returned to Japan to further her career. Despite having trained as a stained-glass artist, she wanted to create large floor-to-ceiling panels, involving the beauty of mouth-blown glass but without the many limitations of working with lead. She had always loved the sparkling effects seen when the cut edge of glass is exposed to light, and eventually she discovered a soft transparent tape that would bond cut glass pieces on one edge – just 3mm (0.1in) thick – leaving the other edge exposed to the light. With this method she has achieved the perfect technique to express her vision, as well as enabling her to create a totally engaging experience for her clients.

Commissioning a work from Yamamoto is a truly communal experience. The artist likes to include her clients in as much of the experience of creating the end product as possible, with the result that when the panels are finally installed they belong to all those involved.

1

1 EGG OF THE EARTH, Hamamatsu, Japan, 2004. Architect: Masahito Nagata. The picture shows the entranceway of a company headquarters. The simple pattern is made from thousands of small glass pieces in tones of blues and greens, with darker blues toward the base.

2 MACHIDA CHURCH, Tokyo, Japan, 2001. The nine panels of this window are made up of thousands of different tones of amber glass fragments, recovered from the original church – simple, and very responsive to sunlight.

3 CHAPEL, SEIGAKUIN UNIVERSITY, Saitama, Japan, 2004. Architect: Hisao Koyamo. The detail shows how the panel is built up of small squares of coloured glass with spaces filled with letters, made by the students from strips of glass, to create a Biblical text.

4 CHAPEL Eight frameless panels, mounted in channels top and bottom, create a contemporary frameless "window" that fits the language of the building and matches the style of exterior glazing.

2

3

Firstly Yamamoto prepares a design, then much of the operation of assembling and bonding the tiny pieces of glass onto the base layer is undertaken by the client – often a school or a church. Many are apprehensive, whether of the difficulty, the responsibility, or the required precision. Yet in the conquest of such fears lies the process of creating art that belongs to many.

When glass is first cut it is actually fractured, or broken, along a straight line, but the edge, if unpolished, has a movement and life of its own. By placing all these fragments of glass onto their sides so that the light can pass through the fractured edges, Yamamoto creates windows that shimmer and glitter in sunlight, so that as one moves past them they are constantly sparkling. Because of this her designs are very simple and restrained in the use of colour, allowing the light passing through the glass to be the dominant effect.

4

1

ELEVATOR LOBBY, Hong Kong Financial Centre, 2004. This enormous back-lit glass feature is made up of eight separate walls, each with 42 panels of hand-painted and laminated low-iron glass.

ELEVATOR LOBBY
As is so often the way in architectural work, it is the detailing of the bronze-plated fixings, designed with the interior designer, that help to create this powerful overall effect.

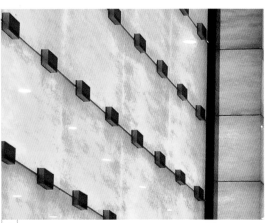

2

Hong Kong artist Eddy Chan has created a studio with enormous skills in almost every aspect of glass creation, ranging from slumping and fusing glass through to painting and laminating glass with resins.

As the process of laminating glass has evolved in recent years it has become possible to achieve completely new effects with the materials available. In the Architecture section we saw how "pigmented lamination" is becoming more and more widespread, while here we see how studios can use advances in technology to paint onto glass and then seal the effects permanently between two layers of glass, with resulting safety advantages and the protection of the painted surface from damage.

Eddy Chan works closely with architects and interior designers to create decorative features that add to interiors. In addition he has been a huge innovator, continually experimenting with new techniques, helping other designers to realize their ideas, and pushing the frontiers of what can be achieved. Being Chinese, Chan approaches his work from a different aesthetic viewpoint to those artists trained in a more Western or European culture. Yellows, reds, and golds are a central part of his instinctive palette, provoking one to realize how comparatively little we see these colours in Western art.

Perhaps because Chan's roots are far from the European tradition of stained glass, fired enamels are not his preferred method of putting colour on glass. China has a huge tradition of hand-painting and a great skills base to draw from, so much of his work uses special resin paints on glass, which is then sealed inbetween two layers of glass. Additional effects, such as sandblasting and acid-etching, are often added later to the outer layer – as seen in the residential screen shown below.

3   **SCREEN**, private residence, Regalia Bay, Hong Kong, 2004. The back-lit screen is made up of three panels, each 1 x 2.5m (3 x 8ft), mounted in front of a mirror.

1 **PRIVATE SWIMMING POOL**, London, 2004. The four panels are back-lit with a Lumitron centrally controlled LED-based lighting system that is 30mm (1.2in) deep.

Most artists have a style that is unique to them, or nearly so, but young Cypriot-born artist Yorgos Papadopoulos has more than just a style – by his mid-20s he had developed a completely new and unique technique. In 1999 Papadopoulos completed a two-year postgraduate course in glass-working at London's prestigious Royal College of Art. Yet already he has moved on to new developments, leaving others to pick up on and be influenced by the work he has done so far.

Glass is a volatile and potentially fragile medium. It can shatter and break, or explode violently, much to the chagrin of those working with the material. Using this property of glass to his advantage, Papadopoulos usually starts the execution of his panels by hammering away at large sections until specific areas have been beaten into a fractured pulp. Then he starts the process of rebuilding his controlled chaos. Having shattered one layer of glass in carefully pre-planned shapes, he fills the cavities he

has created with colours. Having cleaned away the ensuing mess, he then laminates another fresh piece of glass over the top, creating a beautiful piece of triple-laminated glass with a seriously molested interior. The results have a natural, organic feeling to them that speak of fracturing, exploding tensions, growth, and movement. His colours tend to be fairly restrained; the results are undeniably beautiful.

Papadopoulos has the confidence not to sit on his techniques but to broadcast them to the world in the sure knowledge that he has plenty of other ideas. Now in his early 30s, he claims to be moving on to something new. Technique is only a means to an end; art is not created by technique, and Papadopoulos has demonstrated an unusual combination of artist creativity and imaginative use of skills and craftsmanship.

2

3

"GROVE", Canary Wharf, London, England, 2005. An installation based on the symbol of the olive tree. The panels create something like a maze, with different pieces seeming to be parts of a fragmented whole.

"GROVE" These detailed images show the fractures in the glass and the way the colours are cleverly trapped inside the fractures, darker at the centres and moving outward in organic, almost geological, forms – more like stains or blemishes than controlled painting.

4

Chris Wood initially studied furniture design, but an interest in light led her to explore the physical and visual qualities of glass. She then went on to study glass at the Royal College of Art in London, where she worked on large-scale projects dealing with light and space. After leaving the RCA she worked for a time as a project manager, organizing installations for the UK-based glass sculptor Danny Lane.

Wood creates experimental installation work for exhibition. This exploratory approach is a vital element of her practice, advancing her visual vocabulary and her understanding of light and its interaction with glass. Informed by this she also produces work to commission for interior and architectural situations. The distinctive feature of her work is its physical simplicity, which is contrasted with its visual complexity. Wood has very focused ideas and goals regarding her work.

1

1 **SACKVILLE HOUSE**, near Cambridge, England, 2004. This view of the hanging feature shows some of the 48 panels of dichroic glass in various colours that cast light onto the white surrounding walls in all directions, depending on the angle of the sunlight.

2 **SACKVILLE HOUSE** This elliptical hanging feature, measuring 3.2m (10ft) at its widest diameter, hangs in the central atrium of a small local administrative office building and health centre.

2

3

4

3 4 5 6

"LADDER OF LIGHT", Papworth Hospital, near Cambridge, England, 2003. This feature was designed to create an artwork for the large blank wall in the stairwell of a new extension to the hospital. Commissioned on a limited budget, the work is a simple structure of suspended panels of dichroic glass, which, when illuminated by natural or artificial light, project changing geometric forms of coloured light onto the opposite and adjacent walls.

5

6

The projects shown on these pages feature dichroic glass, a material that is now widely used by glass artists because of its kinetic qualities. Dichroic glass is not easy to describe. It manifests as two colours, one transparent, the other reflective, at opposite ends of the colour sprectrum. The glass may transmit blue light in transparent mode and reflect red in the opposite direction in reflective mode, depending on where the higher light level comes from. Dichroic glass is expensive, but can be purchased in many different pairs of colours. The colours given off are very pure and dynamic.

Wood creates minimalist structures that support pure and simple arrangements of glass that interact with natural or projected light to create complex and changing patterns of light. The works are experiential in nature, engaging the viewer directly with the optical kinetics produced by the shifting position of the viewer and the varying quality of the light source.

Spanish artist José Fernández Castrillo has discovered and developed a method of bringing his glass designs into reality that is unlike anything any other artist is doing. He has evolved techniques with a CNC (computer-controlled) polishing machine that no one else has even tried, let alone developed to this degree of precision and virtuosity. His panels embody the curious contradiction of clearly being one-off works of art, yet having a quality of precision in their execution that could be achieved only with digitally-controlled machinery creating the many component parts.

Like many artists, Castrillo started by making leaded-glass panels in the late 1970s. He moved on to "dalle de verre" (rocks of glass embedded in concrete), and ended up making exquisite minimalist panels from float glass. Because of his commitment to exhibiting his work in art galleries he was compelled to develop ways of making autonomous, free-standing pieces that did not require back-lighting and could easily be housed in a gallery, viewed from all directions, walked around, and picked up and taken home. The basic material was a sheet of plain float glass, for which he designed simple but elegant "legs". Onto these panels, often measuring 80 x 80cm (32 x 32in), he could paint, sandblast away, acid-etch, and bond things. This method introduced a simplicity to his works, giving them the quality of minimalist paintings. Thus, over some years, he developed the techniques that have become integral to his ongoing artistic language.

Castrillo has been making windows and partition screens for buildings for at least 20 years. They are very architectural pieces, with the virtue of embodying a combination of minimalism and energy. Some of his works have been very colourful, and others without any colour at all. But they all have a highly tactile, sensuous quality where, because the glass is so perfectly smooth and aligned, it seems to demand to be touched and felt.

1   **"RIU" ("RIVER")**, Xerta, Tarragona, Spain, 2004, 6.6 x 2.4m (22 x 8ft). This screen is a classic example of Castrillo's work. His projects often comprise an interesting mix of dynamism and serenity.

2

3

4

"RAIGS X" ("X-RAY"),
Barcelona, Spain, 1997.
This detail from a panel made for
a doctor's clinic shows the three-
dimensional quality of the work,
the polishing of shaped pieces
in perfect parallel lines, and the
different unique profiles in a
mixture of clear and matt surfaces.

"RUSHES", private
residence, Canterbury,
England, 2003, 3.2 x 2.4m
(10 x 8ft). This monotone screen,
weighing 350kg (770lb), was
installed as a single panel of glass.
The sun falls on it in the morning
and evening, casting refracted
colours on floor and walls.

"CONCEPTO ESPACIAL"
("SPACE CONCEPT"),
Terrassa, Barcelona, Spain, 2003,
2.1 x 2.1m (7 x 7ft). The detail
from this panel shows the variety
of different profiles Castrillo can
create, as well as the different
colours in small elements that
are delicately placed.

5 **"ENCUENTRO ENTROPICO" ("ENTROPIC MEETING")**, private residence, Alella, Barcelona, Spain, 1999, 5.2 x 4.5m (17 x 15ft). This shows part of a staircase feature installed in a private house. The piece is made up of five panels of external glazing, going around a corner.

Tom Patti has been working with glass for 35 years. A graduate of New York's Pratt Institute, with a Master's in Industrial Design and Architectural Theory, Patti became involved, in the 1960s, with E.A.T. (Experiments in Art & Technology), a project co-founded with Robert Rauschenburg to promote collaboration between artists and engineers. Patti has been engaged constantly with the technical boundaries of working with glass, making small-scale objects for exhibition in galleries as well as doing architectural commissions on a large scale. All of his work is made in his own studio, where he is involved with every stage of the creation and assembly.

Patti's most recently completed projects include a series of five monolithic panels suspended above a circular atrium in a new apartment complex on the Lower West Side of Manhattan. The panels are suspended with hinged brackets beneath a clerestory, and lit by a mixture of natural and artificial light. By cutting and mixing different layers of patterned glass, Patti adds textures to the piece, and creates the coloured forms using rectangular shapes of glass and plastic in different colours. Thus the work changes colour as the viewer moves or as the illumination shifts. In the pictures below we see the main areas of the panels as purple and pale blue, whereas in the picture opposite the same areas are cream and purple respectively. One of the virtues of Patti's glass is the way that it creates fabulous patterns of colour on the floors underneath the glass, and on the walls opposite.

The glass feature in the station in Queens, New York, (*see* pp.146–7) is a collaboration between Patti and Fox & Fowle Architects. Patti uses a minimalist form, with formal and regular geometric interruptions, to add drama to the architecture. Because there is no contradiction of language between the architecture and the art, the effect of the coloured forms is to enrich the architecture, the glass, and the experience of the interior space and the cityscape.

1 **"LIGHT MONITOR"**, Morton Square, Greenwich Village, New York, USA, 2004. Depending on the angle of view, the five glass panels appear in particular colours.

2 **"LIGHT MONITOR"** The five panels, each approximately 1 x 3m (3 x 10ft), are made of structural glass, textured glass, and coloured plastics laminated together to create an array of shapes and colours.

1

3

4

3 **"PASSAGES 2004"**, Roosevelt/74th St Station, New York, USA, 2004, 18 x 3.5m (60 x 12ft). This exterior image is a frozen moment, but in life the work changes colour with the light and the viewer's movement.

4 **"PASSAGES 2004"** This detail shows how the ribbed texture adds greatly to the interest of the surfaces of the glass. The colours generated by the different angles of the glass interact with one another.

5

6

5 **"PASSAGES 2004"** This interior view shows the relatively formal design pattern – sympathetic and well integrated with the station's architecture.

6 **"SPECTRAL-LUMA ELLIPSE"**, Museum of Fine Arts, Boston, USA, 2000, 6 x 3m (20 x 10ft). This glass entrance to the museum's Gund Gallery is created using specially manufactured film within the laminated glass, which responds in different ways as light strikes its surface.

Slumped glass still has the potential to awe people, perhaps because the process of heating float glass over a mould suddenly turns a totally artificial and manufactured product into a wonderfully organic and unmechanized one.

Despite this, many slumped-glass factories work to make their products as uniform as possible, so that the material can be bought out of a catalogue to a required size.

Slumped glass can be coloured in various ways. It can be enamelled, using any of the different methods, though there is the minor difficulty that the optimum temperatures at which enamels are fired into the glass are significantly lower than that required for slumping glass – hence colours will behave in unpredictable ways. It can also be coloured using cold colours, either by sandblasting the glass and adding pigments, or by using transparent colours that can be airbrushed onto the glass after the texture is created.

Fusing glass is another process, involving heating several glass layers to much higher temperatures, at which the glass melts sufficiently to fuse together. Coloured glasses are available that are made specifically to be compatible for fusing together.

Glass as a material has become synonymous with a lack of texture, flaws, and incident. The material has become, in a sense, the perfect absence. Nothing is happening, and light passes through uninterrupted – a most unnatural product. However, slumped glass resembles something that has been washed by the sea for centuries and eroded into a more bumpy surface that holds light and allows all sorts of sparkles to form in its crevices and undulations.

ABOVE **EXTERIOR SEATING FEATURE**, Broadgate, London, England, 2003, 90 x 50cm (35 x 20in). Architect: SOM. Textured glass panels with bright polished edges rise up out of the ground. Each panel is 13cm (5in) thick and weighs 130kg (290lb).

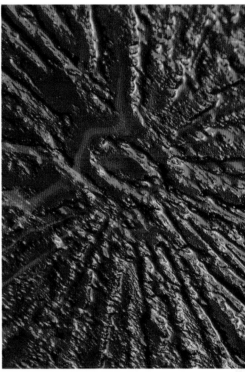

TOP LEFT **PRESIDENTIAL RESIDENCE SYNAGOGUE**, Jerusalem, Israel, 2002: by Mira Maylor. The three windows make up a wall of textured glass that has been sandblasted and hand-painted with cold resin colours, creating a powerful brilliance of incandescent light.

ABOVE **"FOUNTAIN WALL"**, garden of private residence, San Francisco, USA, 1997: by John Lewis. These blocks of glass 30mm (1¼in) thick, were cast by the Californian glass artist. Moulten glass was poured into a graphite mould, creating a texture that matches rough stone.

TOP RIGHT **"OZONE DISC"**, 2000. This detail from a slumped glass panel shows a two-part transparent pigment bonded to a textured glass, creating different reflections and tonal variations.

1

ST CANISIUS CHURCH,
Freiburg, Germany, 1977.
Fused, cast, enamelled glass –
20 years before most glass
artists had even thought of doing
this. For these panels the artist
received the "Exempla-Preis
München 1977" from Max Bill.

German artist Florian Lechner has been working with
slumped, fused, and cast glass since before many current
practitioners were born. The picture above shows his
first major commission in Freiburg: 25-mm (1-in) thick,
rugged, textured glass panels with enamelled colour.
His first big hanging glass sculpture, a great glass
chandelier not shown here, was installed in Regensburg
in 1974. Made of 32 fused and slumped elements, it was
at the time the largest thing of its kind ever installed. In
1982 Lechner installed a huge octagonal glass fountain in
Munich, nearly 7m (23ft) tall, made up of three layers of
slumped and fused glass that were laminated and drilled.

The work used a special technology devised by Lechner –
tested by the Fraunhofer Institute and later patented.

Lechner studied painting for three years in Kassel
and sculpture and painting in Paris, and in the mid-1960s
he spent three years doing specialized studies in
glassmaking, both artistic and industrial. With such
an extensive background of research and intellectual
development it is not surprising that he has been a
pioneer from the beginning, always pushing the medium
to perform beyond its previously accepted boundaries.

Using glass as a hanging sculptural medium is always
challenging. Glass is heavy, in some respects fragile, and

2

**MUNICH RE INSURANCE
2 CO**, London Headquarters,
England, 1988. Floor-to-ceiling
office partitioning with
enamelled areas for prestigious
London offices.

**CHAPEL AT MUNICH
3 AIRPORT**, Germany,
1989/90. Window detail
showing movement similar
to a conductor's motion.

potentially dangerous. The difficulty is to design the
fixings so that the metal does not detract from or
overwhelm the glass. Artists creating unique designs
without large budgets often find this aspect very
challenging. We can see from the sculptures in Weiden
and in Ruuen (see p.152) how successfully Lechner's
own patented methods have resolved such problems.

Like the work of Renato Santarossa (see pp.160–61),
Lechner's designs have been mainly about form and texture,
with colour being an added ingredient. But more recently,
as shown in his glass mobile in Wunsiedel (see p.153), he has
been exploring the use of colour as a central part of his art.

3

4

5

6

4 **COLUMN WITH PRISMS**, Congress Center, Weiden, Germany, 1992. Architect: BDA/DWB. This extraordinarily beautiful piece blends in completely with the style and language of the architecture.

5 **6** **GLASS-LIGHT COLUMN**, Rouen, France, 1995, 11m (36ft) tall. Architect: Yves Couloume. Made with 36 prisms of glass, this sculpture stands in the central station of Rouen.

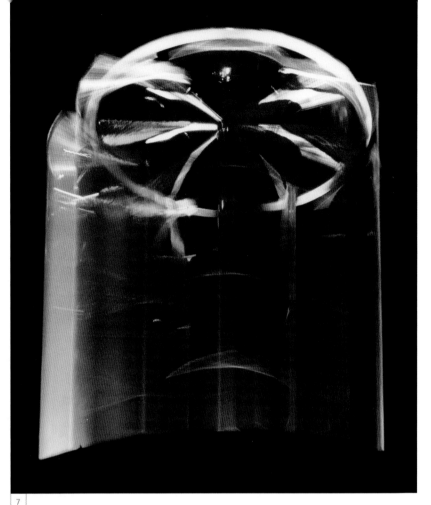

7

8

7 | **GLASS, LIGHT GAME**, Wunsiedel, Germany, 2003, 3.4m (11ft) tall. This shows the sculpture spinning in the night-time, the colours changing as they mix with each other and spin on their own axes.

8 | **GLASS, LIGHT GAME** The sculpture is based entirely on colour and movement, but without any movement in the shape or texture of the glass itself.

Though French in origin, Thierry Boissel has been living and working in Munich for more than 15 years. He started out as a stained-glass artist, but was always dissatisfied with this medium as a language for contemporary architecture. It was a moment of revelation when he first encountered fused glass. But that was only the beginning of a ten-year process of discovery and experiment. For him, the way that slumped and fused glass modulates and transforms light coming through glass was the key. It is the variety and the subtlety of the textures that can be achieved, and how each one shifts the way light enters a space, that became his main interest.

In the project shown here Boissel is responding to the specific architectural context, and thinking in Bauhaus terms of rectilinear forms, and of interacting and overlapping rectangles and colours. But he is equally at home in a Gothic environment, where the rugged,

textured nature of slumped glass works very successfully with the surrounding stonework. Slumped glass is an excellent medium in Gothic buildings that are looking for glass to keep them enclosed while allowing in light, without challenging the language and medium of the original construction – as happens when contemporary float glass, with its perfectly flat surface, is introduced into eroded stone apertures.

Despite the techniques that are available, such as printing with enamels and digital printing, Boissel is clear that, for him at least, these have no place in art. Rather than screen-printed enamels, he prefers the hand-application of colour. Boissel is a purist as he believes that the interference of the machine or of mechanized processes should be kept out of the creation of art.

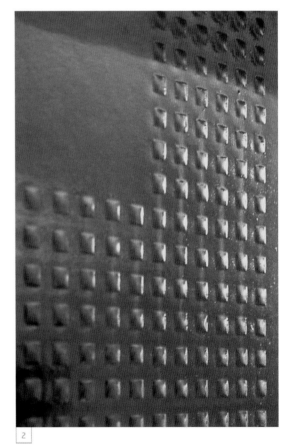

1

2

1 **FUNERAL PARLOUR**,
Neubiberg, Germany, 2000.
Detail showing part of toughened
glass sliding door panel.

2 **FUNERAL PARLOUR**
Detail showing slumped
squares with smooth background
texture, partially silver-stained.

3 **FUNERAL PARLOUR**
This shows a typical
interaction of colour,
rectangles, and textures,
which work with the rectangular
forms of the architecture.

1 "RETURN TO
THE COSMOS",
Mexico City, 2005, 3 x 11m
(8 x 36ft). This photograph
shows the base of architect
Ariel Blomberg's new building
in the Paseo Reforma, Mexico
City. The external cladding
is all low-iron (white) glass,
contrasting with Quagliata's
back-lit feature tucked inside.

2 "RETURN TO
THE COSMOS"
The computer-controlled back-
lighting of the glass feature
increases or decreases depending
on day or night conditions.

Italian-born artist Narcissus Quagliata is the master
of the technique of fusing glass, and is one of the few
architectural artists who work with fused glass on a large
scale. Quagliata is no stranger to large commissions.
Although he lives in Mexico City, he has taken
commissions all over the world, particularly in the United
States, Italy, and the Far East. He has executed many
large glass art projects entirely at his own expense,
with the expectation of selling them through galleries
or exhibitions at a later time. He also does many smaller
works of 1–2sqm (3–7sqft) specifically for galleries and
collectors who wish to purchase his prolific output.

The project shown here, "Return to the Cosmos", is
in many ways a merging of these two modes of operation.
It has been designed specifically with the site in mind,
but reflects a completely autonomous expression of
Quagliata's creative instincts at that time. He describes
the piece as a meditation on the unstable and fleeting

nature of our place in the universe – joy and sorrow
merged together. The work is sited in a powerful
architectural setting, with the austere white building in
extreme contrast with the bursting, swirling colour of
Quagliata's glass. The location of the panel under the
overhanging roof provides shade from the bright sunlight,
and helps create the impression of a burning jewel in
the heart of this soaring tower.

The glass used in this work is the fusable glass
produced by the manufacturer Bullseye, here used in
sheet form together with various frits and "stringers".
Quagliata mixes the techniques most commonly used in
blown glass to build up the layers of colour and texture.

1

2

4

5

6

3

3 **"RETURN TO THE COSMOS"** The 33 panels of fused glass express a typical Quagliata "Cosmos" painting, with brilliant galaxies colliding in a fusion of technical drama.

4 **"RETURN TO THE COSMOS"** The surface texture of this piece begins to be seen in the detailed images, and the glass appears far more transparent.

5 **"RETURN TO THE COSMOS"** Because this glass is fused in two main firings, the artist adds new layers at a late stage, continually over-painting the surface.

6 **"RETURN TO THE COSMOS"** Close up, this piece loses its almost airbrushed look and becomes tactile and mysterious, with different colours emerging from within the glass.

Tomasz Urbanowicz has the advantage over most glass artists of having graduated as an architect, while also having studied stained glass. He and his wife Beata, who is also a qualified architect, founded their own studio in 1987 in Wroclaw, Poland, to make glass art for architecture. Despite having started in stained glass Urbanowicz became increasingly involved in developing the techniques of moulding, fusing, and pigmenting glass. His work has a rugged earthiness that is quite distinctive, and different from the textures that are more commonly seen in slumped glass.

It is curious how the very boldness of the medium makes the analysis of the design element difficult. Much of Urbanowicz's glass looks as if its texture simply arrived that way by means of some natural process. Sometimes the colours, as in the Holstein Brewery project shown below, look as if they are more an accidental by-product of the process than a carefully calculated colour scheme that works with the space. In his work it is often the details that the eye fails to perceive easily that are the secret ingredient that gives his work that indefinable quality of excellence. In the Holstein Brewery it is the way the bar glass appears to hang in front of the base unsupported. In the screen called "Catch a Wind", the glass appears to stand on the polished floor, the two surfaces meeting seamlessly. Such detailing reveals the architectural training of the artist.

Tomasz Urbanowizc has done sculptures, mouldings for architectural details, classical columns, semicircular window recesses, and cast stonework. His work involves all the skills of the painter, the sculptor, and the architectural glass artist, and is almost evenly split between private and public commission. Now he is increasingly working beyond the borders of Poland.

1 | **HOLSTEIN BREWERY HEADQUARTERS**, Hamburg, Germany, 2000. The bar and the screen show the beautiful colours that Urbanowicz added to their thick, boldly sculpted glass. The bar glass is lit with down-lighters, and fixed to hang from the top surface.

1

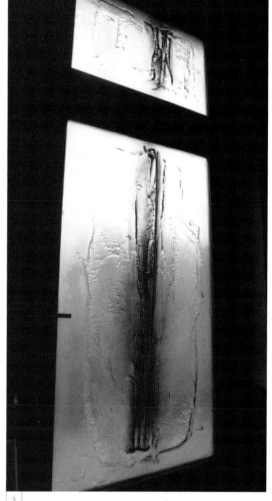

2 **"CATCH A WIND"**, private house, Wroclaw, Poland, 2003, 3m (10ft) tall. Panels of moulded glass are fixed so as to emerge seamlessly from the floor and ceiling, separated by a sandblasted glass doorway.

3 **DOOR PANEL**, Hotel Erania, Kolobrzeg, Poland, 2004. This beautifully pigmented panel shows the range of colours that Urbanowicz can achieve. The results seem organic, as if carved by erosion over centuries.

4 **"HOT SUN"**, private residence, Poznan, Poland, 2003, 2.7m (9ft) tall. This panel has the appearance of a prehistoric carving into a rockface made of glass. The delicate pigmentation gives the piece a warm glow.

5 **BALUSTRADES IN A PALACE**, near Warsaw, Poland, 2003. Thick chunks of glass have been sunk into deep channels to create a continuous, frameless balustrade.

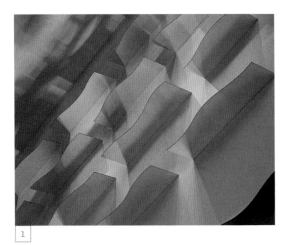

1

1

"GLOBAL GATE 1",
Dusseldorf, Germany,
2001. This wall-mounted glass
artwork for an entrance lobby
mixes three-dimensional
elements with a simple shaped
panel of painted laminated glass.

2 **"GLOBAL GATE 1"**
This picture shows the
16 "shelves" of dichroic glass,
casting coloured forms onto
the rear wall in transmitted
and reflected light.

2

Renato Santarossa has been working with glass for
45 years. Although Italian by origin, he has lived in
Dusseldorf, Germany, for many years. He is one of
those few architectural artists who, as well as doing
commissioned works, also creates autonomous
sculptures and installation pieces for exhibition
in galleries both in Germany and farther afield.

Santarossa experiments not only with basic float
glass, trying different ways to cut or score the surface
or edges of the glass, but also with industrial products,
such as glass rods or tubes, exploring different lighting
effects. "The question is how to make visible the
transparency, which you can only do at the same moment
that you destroy the transparency. In other words you
need to destroy the glass to make the glass visible. When
I realized this ... I began to understand Lucio Fontana,
what he meant when he slashed his canvases."

The work shown here is typically eclectic in its style
and use of materials. He is constantly exploring what
glass will do when subjected to this or that lighting, or
fracturing or moulding of its surface. For much of his
career he avoided the use of colour entirely, feeling that
the unique properties of the material were obscured by
colour, and that by avoiding it he was forcing himself to
discover what the material itself could achieve. But more
recently he has allowed himself to be liberated from
such constraints, though colour is still applied delicately,
or in the case of dichroic glass, used because it is its
relationship with light that is the intriguing element.

Santarossa's career has been greatly helped by the
patronage of churches, but in recent years it has been
more and more the secular market of office buildings,
banks, and other prestigious environments that has
enabled him to create the large wall-mounted or free-
standing sculptures that are of greatest interest to him.

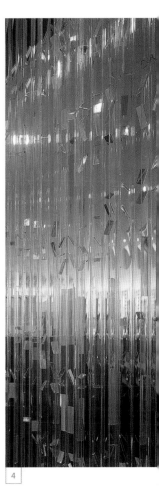

3 **GLASS SCULPTURE**,
National Bank, Essen,
Germany, 2002, 3.5m (12ft)
tall. The sculpture is made
up of hollow glass tubes
with dichroic glass inside.

4 **GLASS SCULPTURE**,
Stadtsparkasse, Singen,
Germany, 2000. A 6-m (20-ft)
long wall, 3m (10ft) tall, made
of densely packed glass tubes
with small strips of dichroic
glass creating flowing forms.

Sandblasting glass is a process by which the surface of the glass is abraded by grains of sand driven on a jet of compressed air. When lightly done, this frosts or peppers the surface of glass; when done with intense pressure and a highly abrasive material it is possible to cut right through thick glass and to shape its edges.

Carving glass, which is the act of shaping the glass into relief shapes, is very akin to sculpture – the glass being eaten away to create modelled shapes, like the relief carving seen on mouldings. Lighting is important with sandblasted glass because everything is essentially white: if the light falls correctly the moulded shapes reveal the shadows that express the form.

A skilled craftsperson can create detailed three-dimensional shapes and textures that respond superbly to lighting. The examples shown here focus on sandblasted glass when used with colour. Different artists and craftspeople have their own methods of "painting" the glass, and most will refer somewhat opaquely to "varnishes", "resins", and "enamels". There are also "cold" glass paints available, both oil- and water-based, which can create wonderful results on carved glass, where the varying depths and textures in the glass create different tonalities of colour in the "varnish". The varnish bonds superbly to the abraded surface and virtually restores the glass to shining transparency. These materials are not as permanent as fired enamels, but are surprisingly durable and UV-resistant, and it is often possible to put the decorated surface inside a sealed unit so that nothing can damage the surface.

Sandblasting is, in many ways, the most difficult glass-working technique. In the absence of good lighting the work can be a disaster. But, when used skilfully, it is amazing what can be achieved.

ABOVE **CARVED SHELL**, Radisson Edwardian Hotel, Heathrow, London, England, 2002: by John Williams. This carved glass shell is part of a bar-top. The shell has dichroic film behind, creating the rippling golds, blues, and greens.

OPPOSITE LEFT **MARUNOUCHI BUILDING**, Tokyo, Japan, 2002: by Shelagh Wakely. This silver tree has been carved into the rear face of the glass and filled with silver paint. The tree becomes an image of reflected light.

OPPOSITE TOP RIGHT **"EUPHONY"**, Ted Stevens Anchorage International Airport, Alaska, USA, 2004: by Warren Carther. This detail shows shapes cut out of glass with a sandblaster, textures carved into glass, and colours painted onto the abraded surface.

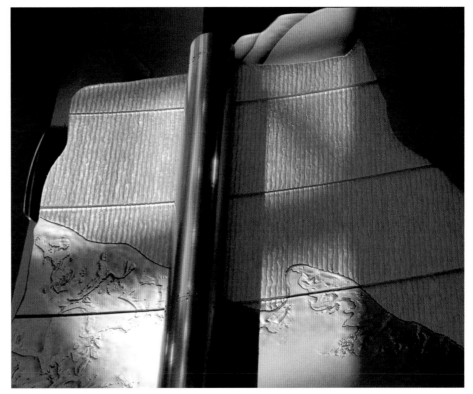

ABOVE **THE LABORATORY HEALTH CLUB**, London, England, 1999, 3 x 1.5m (10 x 5ft): by Pip Tunstall. One of three double-glazed panels, deeply carved to create contrasting different textures and then airbrushed and hand-painted with coloured resins.

ABOVE **"POH'S GOLDFISH"**, private residence, London, England, 2003: by John Williams. This detail of a carved and hand-painted goldfish illustrates the rich colours and transparent luminosity that can be achieved with hand-painted cold resins.

By the time he graduated from art school Warren Carther had already decided he wanted to work with glass. He went on to study glass-blowing in New York and later in California. But, by the time he had graduated in 1977, he realized that glass-blowing could never offer the potential to build the enormous walls of glass he was imagining.

He returned to his native Canada to begin developing the techniques that would eventually enable him to achieve his goal. He considered working with stained glass, but quickly understood the intrinsic limitations of a medium so lacking in innate structural strength. But by working with large sheets of plain float glass, Carther realized that anything was possible. By using unusually thick and costly glass Carther bypassed the difficulties caused by the supposed fragility of the medium. At such thickness glass is considered structural even after it has had several millimetres removed from it in various places.

Now in his own studio, Carther works with several different sandblasting units, with different degrees of abrasive materials, enabling him both to carve enormous chunks out of the glass and to execute all the delicate, fine-sand techniques his works require.

Carther has experimented with numerous methods of adding colour to the abraded surface: rubbing in and airbrushing translucent pigments; bonding dichroic glass as an interior layer; and even using metallic colours, which, being quite reflective, tend to manifest as varied colours, depending upon lighting.

Carther seems to move from one enormous commission to another. His Hong Kong triptych "Chronos" formed a total of 360sqm (3,900sqft) of glass, weighing 25 tonnes, while his Anchorage Airport project (*see* p.167) is of a similar scale. His technique of stacking curved glass panels on top of one another enables him to achieve enormous height with a minimum of structural support, although in fact his steel structures only add to the beauty of the sculptures. Carther has broken new ground, working with time-honoured techniques but with a completely new agenda and vision.

1

1 **"VESTIGE"**, Lincoln House, Hong Kong, 1999, 4.75 x 7.25m (15 x 24ft). This wall-mounted work forms the central piece of Carther's enormous "Chronos" trilogy.

2 **"VESTIGE"** The work has copper-plated structural support. Computer-controlled back- and front-lighting allows the dichroic glass element to go through dramatic colour changes.

3

4

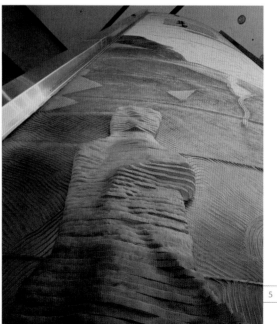

5

3 "APPROACH OF TIME", Lincoln House, Hong Kong, 1999, 3.75 x 13m (12 x 43ft). The final work in the "Chronos" trilogy expresses with its huge height a sense of optimism as it rises towards the future.

4 "PRAIRIE BOY'S DREAM", One Canada Centre, Winnipeg, Canada, 1994, 3.75 x 11m (12 x 36ft). Each of the two towers has 17 curved glass panels 60cm (24in) high, with dichroic glass bonded to the rear surface.

5 "PRAIRIE BOY'S DREAM" Detail from the "front" side, showing layers of glass cut into shapes and bonded to the background glass and frosted white, representing the impact of man on the landscape.

6 **"EUPHONY"**, Ted Stevens Anchorage International Airport, Alaska, USA, 2004. A cluster of tall curved glass sculptures made from 19-mm (0.7-in) thick curved glass panels. Note the contrast in the copper/russet colours in the centre of the panels. Metallic pigments give off different colours depending upon the direction of the light source.

7 **"EUPHONY"** Nine free-standing carved glass towers, each about 8.5m (28ft) tall, spanning a total of 43m (141ft), guard the entrance to the departures lounge at Alaska's main airport.

6

7

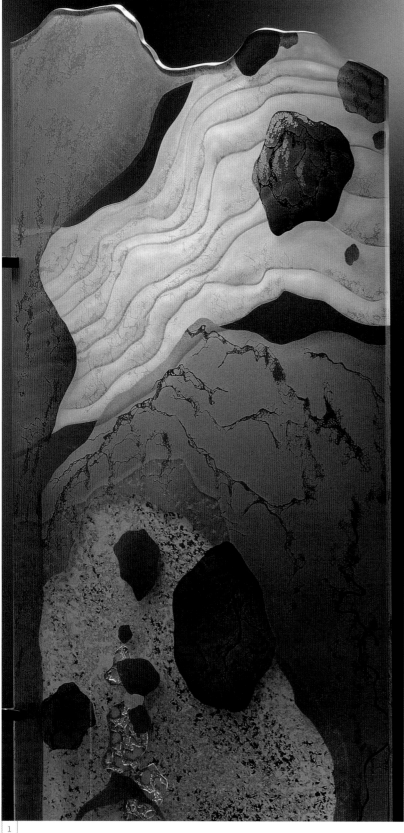

Markian Olynik is a craftsman who works in Vancouver, Canada, making commissions, screens, and free-standing pieces for galleries, collectors, and for corporate and commercial clients. Like many people working in glass Olynik is largely self-taught. In the late 1970s he began exploring how best to blend sandblasting techniques with pigmentation of one sort or another. He experimented with enamel paints but found them limiting, partly because, by their very opacity, they fight against the nature of glass. Olynik then started working with lacquers and varnishes and found that these can retain the translucence or even the transparency of the glass with potentially brilliant colours and tremendous durability.

Working with materials over many years, solving problems, achieving certain textures and effects, is a process of endlessly learning tricks and techniques. Sandblasting, which may involve going right through the glass and shaping its edges, is the initial phase. Most glass panels are at least 12mm (0.5in) and often 19mm (0.7in) thick, so the carving into the glass can be as much as 4–8mm (0.2–0.3in) deep, moulding the form of the object to become as tactile as possible. Most often the glass will then be toughened, which can be a risk as sometimes glass explodes when being toughened, particularly if the angles and edges created are too sharp.

Olynick then starts to add the colours, perhaps with an airbrush, by rubbing into the etched surface, or by floating them into a crevice in the glass. Sometimes the colour may be removed with acid and sandblasted, creating new textures and effects to the surface of both the glass and the pigmentation. Finally, the colour and parts of the etching may have clear lacquer applied, giving an additional texture and feel to the surface of the material. It is the interplay of the matt surfaces and textures against the shiny transparency of the lacquer finishes that is part of the beauty of these pieces.

1 **"EARTH SERIES: CANYON"**, Vancouver, 2001. Detail from one panel of a triptych screen, 1.8 x 2m (6 x 6.5in), showing the shaped edges, deep carved contours, and various varnish treatments.

2 **"GLASS FOUNTAIN"**, Blue Horizon Hotel Lobby, Vancouver, Canada, 2000, 6m (20ft) high. The sculpture is made from carved, painted, and lacquered 12-mm (0.5-in) toughened glass.

1

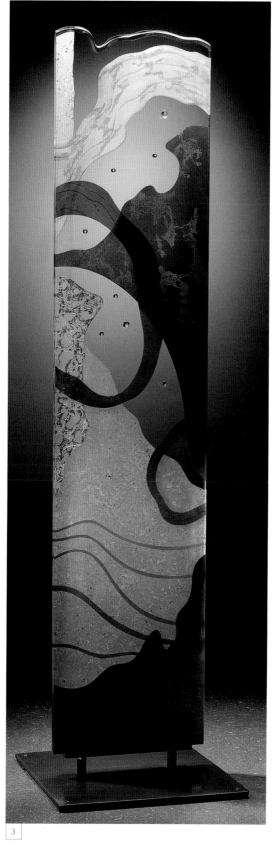

3

3 **"MONOLITH: OCEAN"**,
private collection,
Vancouver, Canada, 2003,
2m (6.5ft) tall. Free-standing
panel in toughened glass. Textures
carved into the glass contrast
with the airbrushed colours.

2

Andreas Horlitz did not start out as an architectural artist – his initial training and interests were in photography and design. Horlitz had his first one-man exhibition in 1978, and since then has been regularly exhibiting works of one sort or another. In 1986 he was appointed visiting lecturer in photography at Cologne University. From that time Horlitz has been creating exhibition pieces based on light boxes. The works have become increasingly complex, playing with images, mirrors, glass, light, and projection. Inevitably, such a focus on how images, light, and glass interact, as well as the discipline of designing and building installations for exhibition spaces, has brought about a particular understanding of how light and glass can work together to create installations in architecture.

"Text DNA" is a 55-m (180-ft) long band of sandblasted mirror, backlit with neon tubes (shown below). It is an excellent example of how a small area of glass can "fill" a large area of wall. The work might appear to be a simple piece to execute, but one suspects there were hidden complexities in arranging for a continuous installation that merges so seamlessly with the white wall, with no fixings and no joins visible.

"Index", Horlitz's glass and light feature for a jobcentre near the Harz mountains in southern Germany, is a beautifully intriguing work that functions from a distance as a simple column of light piercing the building. However, as the viewer approaches the building and eventually enters, the light box becomes increasingly kinetic – a shimmering glow of flickering light.

Horlitz's work is very diverse, but is largely based around the interplay of photography and light. However, as we see in these entirely abstract architectural installations, he has learned how to exploit the properties of glass and light, without the use of photography, in the most minimal way, and to huge effect.

1

2

1 **"TEXT DNA"**, Uniplan International offices, Kerpen-Koln, Germany, 1998. This detail shows how the mirror has been sandblasted away to leave a glowing matt surface that contrasts with the shiny mirror.

2 **"TEXT DNA"** The work is an apparently simple strip of sandblasted mirror, back-lit with neon lights.

3 **"INDEX"**, jobcentre, Sangerhausen, Germany, 1999. This work features three double-sided light boxes, visible from both inside and outside the building, created with a mixture of glass, mirrors, sandblasting, and internal lights.

3

4

5

4 5 **"INDEX"** From up close, the work is a narrow column of flickering light. The glass is made up of horizontal lines of sandblasted and clear glass.

There are five major categories of film in current use: etched, coloured, digitally printed, dichroic, and holographic film. With the exception of holographic film, which is best applied within a laminate, these are all thin layers of different types of plastic that can be applied to glass.

One great advantage of applied film is that it can be temporary: the film may be removed and replaced with a new image relatively easily. But when used in the correct circumstances, film applications can be remarkably durable. I have seen film used on the exterior of buildings that is still there a decade or more later; I have also seen film applied to frameless glass doors, and not be peeling at the edges after many years. The secret with film application is that the adhesive must be given sufficient time to bond. Some films can even be laminated within two layers of glass, creating a completely permanent image, protected on both sides.

However, the fact that film is only an application is also a disadvantage. There is no texture, no penetration of the base material: it is temporary, and can be relatively easily scraped, cut, or damaged in some way. Hence location is a crucial factor when using a film application.

Transparent films are available in many different colours. These can be built up in layers, mixing colours to create tertiary blends, and they can be mixed with etched film to create translucent as well as transparent colours. Digitally printed films offer a much simpler method of achieving a result. Anyone well versed in graphic design or computer-based design can attempt to use digitally printed film, although, as always when working with glass, the fact that the base medium is transparent and not reflective like white paper does introduce complications that can create havoc with the best-laid plans.

Inevitably these film techniques are the most tempting for artists who are not experienced in working with glass, since the design process is either essentially computer-driven or basically a reproductive process.

ABOVE **FINANCIAL SERVICES AGENCY**, London, England, 2004: by Kirsty Brooks. The image shows how film can easily be replaced in the case of a revised interior (*see* the original version on p. 176).

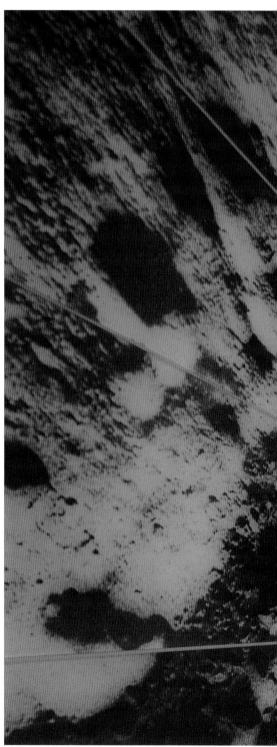

ABOVE **"TIME AND TIDE"**, Plantation Place, London, 2005: by Declan O'Carroll and Arup Associates. This 41 x 6m (134 x 20ft) backlit screen is made from printed film laminated between two layers of 12-mm (½-in) low-iron glass, with an anti-reflective low-acid external finish. The rear of the panels are printed with white enamel, diffusing the LED lighting at the top and bottom.

RIGHT **HOLOGRAPHIC FILM**, Dortmund, Germany, 1999. These six pictures, made by the company GLB, are all images of the same panel of glass, showing how holographic film sandwiched between two layers of glass can reflect different colours.

Born in Cork, Ireland, Kevin Todd explores the interaction of science and art. His early training was in engineering and design drafting, but his inexhaustible curiosity and constant research have kept him in touch with advancing technologies. In the 1990s he began to teach information technology, photography, print media, and digital art, each offering new opportunities to teach and to learn.

Now based in Australia, Todd exhibits globally and is continually involved in exhibitions, curatorial projects, residencies, collaborations, and public art projects. The two projects shown here illustrate his interest in working with digitally created images realized in translucent films and laminated between glass.

The CSIT project, shown below right, was printed on film using an electrostatic process and laminated with resin between two layers of glass. This work refers to the atmospheric quality of the subtropical climate of Australia's Sunshine Coast. The images change according

1

2

to the external or internal light, and become particularly transient at dawn and dusk when the balance between internal and external light shifts slowly from one to the other. The two panels partially enclose this large collective space, delineating the external skin and changing the nature of the space itself.

Inala is a western suburb of Brisbane, and although the community is very multiracial, with many overseas-born residents, the name Inala is an aboriginal word meaning "place of winds", or "meeting of winds". The graphic imagery, shown below left, captures this sense of wind, flow, and energy, with the 16 panels unifying the public spaces of the building.

Todd's work is digitally created, but bridges the gap between concept (computer image) and object (the actual artwork). While many of his images appear almost figurative, they are actually abstract images that are entirely computer-generated.

2 **"ATMOSPHERE #1 & #2"**, Cooloola Sunshine Institute of Technical and Further Education (CSIT), Queensland, Australia, 2003. These two panels are each approx. 4 x 6m (13 x 20ft), executed in film laminated between two layers of glass.

British artist Kirsty Brooks has a distinctive vision and style. She has done many different things with glass, including using enamelled, etched, and sandblasted glass, but is particularly skilled at working with film applications. This is perhaps because she is intensely focused on working with photographic and detailed images, often to create abstract three-dimensional textures. The effect of these images, when incorporated in glass, is to make the surface appear softer and less harsh.

Like many of those who pursue photography, Brooks loves to take pictures of textural surfaces: scrunched-up paper, peeling paint, trees, stacked paper, dried mud, shadows on the floor – wherever Brooks goes she sees new images. She feels these simple images of light and shade can be applied to glass, creating whole new surface textures that breathe life into the glass and the space.

In the Whistler Street project, shown below, Brooks worked closely with the architects, who were creating a pair of experimental new-build houses using an unusual cladding material called Cor-ten – a pre-rusted metal whose colours range from orange through to purple. The whole concept of the building was inspired by a particular industrial landscape. Brooks worked closely with the architects and went to visit the area herself to make her own photographic palette.

Brooks' works create subtle, even unassertive, changes in environments. None the less, despite not making strong statements her input completely changes the experience of the space. These applications are appropriate to many different contexts, either back-lit as wall features, or as an applied transparent film on glass, changing the nature of the membrane between the two spaces that the glass is separating. It is because of this innate sense of texture, rather than form, that Brooks is so specifically architectural in her perception of this medium.

1

2

3

3 **WHISTLER STREET**, London, England, 2005. Seen from the outside, this subtle image in film added to a large glass wall provides privacy for the occupier, while not shutting out interior or exterior.

4 WHISTLER STREET
Seen from inside, the images lurking in the digitally printed film suggest things without being explicit, creating a sense of a separation from outside that is sufficient but not exclusive.

5 WHISTLER STREET
With film there are slight shifts of experience as the viewer moves. Sometimes the film can become more defined, as we see in this picture, where the images suddenly seem much clearer.

Jürgen Drewer is a German architectural artist who works
in many different media, including wood, steel, stone,
and glass. In a recent commission he was able to create
a work that combines a vast oil painting on wood with
a large wall of coloured glass, to form one single design.
The two floor-to-ceiling painted surfaces are thus
broken by a glass wall, the complete design moving
from an opaque material to a translucent material
and back again. The vitally important detailing of the
junction between the two enables the materials to
slide into each other quite imperceptibly.

Drewer starts most works by making paintings,
sometimes as collages, sometimes as oil paintings.
Although the resulting designs are completely abstract,
Drewer attempts to respond to the function of the
space in question, to its occupants, the nature of the
architecture, and perhaps also its history. Although he
works in other media, Drewer feels that glass offers the

opportunity to transform spaces in a unique way, partly
because the glass may be visible from two or more
environments, each of which will experience the glass
partition quite differently, but primarily because adding
colour to glass in a room adds new dimensions in a way
that paintings can not.

Over the past few years Drewer has been excited
by developments in techniques and technology. He has
been keen to experiment with a variety of methods, using
everything from digitally printed film to painting and
airbrushing with lacquers, creating his images on glass
by means of stencils. The use of lacquers creates a
particular type of smooth, even surface texture to the
glass. The technique of preparing the design digitally
allows him as much, if not more, control over the final
result as he would have with non-digital techniques,
but at significantly less cost, thereby making the work
more accessible to a wider audience.

2

3

2 **TRANSLUCENT SCREEN**, Volksbank, 2001, 20 x 3.2m (65 x 10ft). This piece comprises digitally printed film covering free-standing glass screens, which enclose the entrance lobby.

3 **TRANSLUCENT SCREEN** The close-up view of the lobby screen shows how Drewer manages to include transparent areas in the designs, adding a contrasting element to the translucent surround.

1

Espen Tollefsen is a Norwegian photographer who has been creating artworks for many years, but the work shown here is his first experience of working with glass.

The interior designer for the new corporate headquarters of a shipping company, Leif Höegh & Co, wanted to use images on glass to enclose the office conference rooms, without compromising the light. The dramatic shifts in the quality of the light in Norway, from summer-time all-day sunshine to almost permanent twilight in winter, posed additional problems for Tollefsen when planning the images. Photographs are usually experienced in static lighting conditions, either as back-lit

features or as reflective paper. These glass walls would be constantly changing in character and expression as the external light changed. Therefore the images are kept pale and light, animated by even the weakest external light, as well as by artificial light sources. The film holds the light in quite unexpected ways, so that, as you walk along the wall, some white sections can appear as anything from shining white, to grey, to almost black. The pale green of the grass images takes on an intense chlorophyllic hue in low evening sunlight.

The digitally printed film has been applied to the glass in more than one layer, giving additional UV protection

2

3

1　**LEIF HÖEGH & CO**, Oslo, Norway, 2005. Close-ups of grass at various angles create this feature wall on the cafeteria floor of the office building.

2　**LEIF HÖEGH & CO** This detail shows how Tollefsen creates abstract impressions from natural forms and phenomena, allowing the photograph to add atmosphere and texture to the space without being the dominant feature.

3　**LEIF HÖEGH & CO** A fuller view of the same wall shows how each panel of glass has a slightly different image of the same subject, rather than simple vistas.

and also removing the matt surface that comes as the light reflects off the ink. Tollefsen used the silicone joints between the glass panels to add time and movement as elements. Rather than using large landscape pictures, each panel is a separate image, some being repeats of the same subject from a slightly different angle, or the same view of water at a different time of day when the currents and wind move the waves at a different angle.

Most of the images in the office building, unlike the grass image shown above, are almost devoid of colour, so that rather than displaying an arresting image they create a sense of space and texture.

Michael Bleyenberg trained as a painter, and has worked as an artist and lecturer for more than 25 years. After moving to Cologne in 1992 he became intrigued by what contemporary technologies might have to offer his art. He became fascinated by aspects of laser technology that seemed to relate centrally to what he had been doing as a painter – exploring the nature of colour and of light. He found the idea that colour can exist simply suspended in mid-air intriguing, transcendent, and liberating. By dividing white light into its spectral colours, a type of foil, originally developed to assist in the control of light and temperature in buildings, can be used to create art forms.

Technically, these "holographic" artworks that Bleyenberg has designed are formed from a "holographic" film laminated between two layers of glass. In some cases, as in the Bonn mural opposite, the rear layer of glass is mirrored, which enables the light to bounce back through the glass and animate the holographic film. Bleyenberg has been working with a scientific team

1 "EYESCAPE XI",
German/Chinese Science Centre, Beijing, China, 2001, 2 x 2m (6.5 x 6.5ft). This holographic artwork appears static, but when the viewer moves it changes its colours, and at times seems almost to vanish completely.

2 "LIGHTKITE",
Bias Bremer Institute for Applied Laser Technology, Bremen, Germany, 2002. This work hangs in a stairwell; two intersecting planes of glass are animated by surrounding lights.

2

3

4

5

"EYEFIRE", DFG, Bonn, Germany, 2000, 5 x 13m (16 x 43ft). A mural in the form of a hologram decorates the side of this scientific institute. This work is mounted as cladding on a concrete wall, with mirrored glass behind.

"EYEFIRE" The work responds entirely to the light that is cast upon it, and will manifest itself differently depending on the direction and nature of the light source.

"EYEFIRE" In daylight, as shown here, the colours are almost the reverse of the dusk picture above. But, as the viewer moves, the colours change and the forms shift.

developing this product since the early 1990s. His role is one of understanding the medium, and then designing forms that the changing colours will adopt.

For the spectator this type of art form can be confusing. It is not possible to perceive the works as an unchanging whole, there being an almost infinite number of manifestations they may adopt. In this sense they are chameleons, changing their colours in response to the environment. This is particularly true when natural light is the activating force, because the variables are so enormous, even if the viewer does not move. Clearly a project such as this curtain wall in Bonn will be perceived differently by those in adjacent offices, by pedestrians or drivers, and by those entering or leaving the building.

Glass art is perhaps the most potent medium in terms of its capacity to transform the experience and atmosphere of an environment. Painting occupies the high ground of fine art as we understand it historically, but I believe the supreme art is glass.

It is interesting to note how poorly glass often works when several artists are let loose on the same space, as has sometimes happened in churches. Unlike in a picture gallery, which can well contain a wide variety of styles, the windows of a building must work together or they barely work at all. In this sense, glass art is an architectural art: it shapes people's experiences of a building, its interior, and its exterior.

Creating a brief

Residential glass art commissions usually arise from the imagination and interests of the house owner, but also frequently reflect the vision of an architect or interior designer. Commissions for public buildings are often inspired by architects, by the building's owner, or by a public body that sponsors art in public spaces.

Regardless of the initiator of the proposal, it is important to define the objectives clearly before talking to a studio, artist, or art consultant – to decide what the glass is there to achieve, on a practical and an aesthetic level. For instance, the glass may have some functional purpose, such as obscuring an ugly outlook, utilizing bricked-up window frames, or enclosing or enhancing a specific space. There may also be commercial objectives. These may include attracting attention to a building, making an environment more welcoming, or creating an ambience in which people will want to stay longer. The glass may be planned as a modest decoration that is responsive to the architecture as a whole, or it may be perceived as a focal point.

Choosing a studio or artist

Regardless of a project's size or sophistication, there are definite benefits, including financial ones, in having access to the skills, resources, and experience of a large studio or a glass specialist. Not many studios have the capacity to manufacture projects using the techniques shown in this book or are capable of large-scale projects. It is therefore important to approach a studio or a consultant with suitable experience to advise on the commission.

If you are contemplating a major commission, seek early advice on the probable overall costs, the practical problems involved, and suitable artists – even if you have a very specific concept in mind.

The best way to gain this type of input is to go to a large studio or a specialist consultant. Alternatively, you may seek out a commercial art consultant who will be able to show you the works of several potentially suitable candidates, but may not be able to offer advice on the technical and practical aspects, including the budget.

As with most aesthetic choices, the final decision on design is often based on very subjective grounds. Sometimes designing a glass project may be an entirely collaborative affair, with input from the architect, the client, and the artist, the result being the fruit of brainstorming by all parties. In such a situation it will be the perception of the potential chemistry that will be the defining factor in choosing whom to employ. Some architects have a single artist with whom they work frequently; some prefer to work with different people for each project; and some work directly with glass consultants or studios that can take their ideas and help to bring them to fruition.

Competitions

A competition can be an effective way of finding a suitable artist. The fees paid to entrants are frequently derisory in terms of the time, expense, and effort involved, so some established artists are reluctant to submit to the stress of such a trial by combat. But competitions are often the route by which younger artists establish themselves and, for clients who do not know what they want, they inexpensively help to generate ideas.

The cost of glass art

The costs will include design and project management; the glass itself; manufacturing the glass to match the design; planning the installation, including manufacturing frames or fittings if required; and installing the completed glass. In addition, thought must be given to lighting. This may not be part of the actual commission, but may add considerably to the overall cost.

It is difficult to make generalizations about cost and value. Some projects are designed in a particular way because the budget is small, yet the result may be hugely successful, often because the financial parameters ensure that the design is simple, direct, and uncluttered. But low budgets increase risk. The result may be predicted with much less certainty because the much-needed samples have not been made and tested on-site or in carefully replicated lighting conditions.

One of the substantial benefits of the switch from using leaded glass to working with float glass is that glass art can become part of the fabric of a building. Thus the costs of the glass itself, the frames, and the installation of the glass are already contained within the budget for the building. The cost of the "art" element is only the cost of the design and the work done to the glass. With more traditional stained glass, the art glass would normally be a secondary glazing, with additional frames, additional installation, and the material itself all part of an add-on cost. The costs are greatly reduced if one works with materials that are part of the structure of the building, .

Frames and fixings

The quality of many aspects of architecture is in the detail. The same is true of architectural glass art. The success of a project often lies in the designing and detailing of the method of installation. Creating a minimum of visible joints and intersections demands much thought in advance. It also demands a high quality of craftsmanship from the manufacturer and builder. Less is often more in terms of time, thought, and eventual cost. But the results more than outweigh these disadvantages.

Lighting

Glass can be tricky to light. If you are dealing with lighting consultants, find out about their experience in working with glass, or do elaborate tests before installation, or build in considerable flexibility so the final location and the precise fixtures can be adjusted after the glass has been installed.

Installation

The moment of installation is often the moment of truth. Glass is, in many ways, an unforgiving medium. It cannot normally be cut down a little or reshaped on-site to correct an inexact fit – it is usually easier to adjust the building than to adjust the glass. It is impossible to take too much care to ensure that the beautiful glass will fit into its intended spot as if it were made for it.

Acid etching
The process of covering the surface of glass with hydrofluoric acid. This technique is used to create a matt translucent surface on "float glass". It is also used to remove the thin layer (less than 1mm) of "flashed" colour from some mouth-blown glass.

Acid polishing
A process of bringing glass back to clear by using a slightly different mixture of acid from that used for etching. It includes sulphuric acid with the hydrofluoric acid.

Antique glass
Flat glass sheets, approximately 600 x 900mm (24 x 35in), made by producing mouth-blown cylinders, cutting down the side while the glass is hot, and flattening them. This process creates glass panels, each of which is very slightly different from all others, with the potential for many different textures and movement in the colours.

Bevels
Polished angles cut into the edges of glass for decorative effect.

Brilliant cutting
The process of using a series of abrasive stones to grind decorative features such as bevelled edges, circles, and V-shapes into the surface of glass.

Carving
Sandblasting using cut masks, usually made from a thick vinyl, that can inscribe lines and shapes into the surface of glass.

Casting glass
The process of heating glass in a mould until it becomes liquid, and then slowly cooling it back into a solid form. This is often done using cullet.

Cavity venting
Creating natural air circulation by using a double skin on the exterior of a building, through which warm air will rise.

Cullet
Broken or scrap glass that is melted to create cast glass. Cullet can be purchased in many different colours and grades.

Dichroic film
A transparent "film" which shows one colour when transmitting light and a different colour when reflecting light. The colours will be from opposite ends of the spectrum and will mix to create many tones when seen from oblique angles. Dichroic film is currently available in only two colours – a purple which reflects yellow, and a blue which reflects red.

Dichroic glass
Glass which shows one colour when transmitting light and a different colour when reflecting light. These colours will be opposites in the spectrum. When seen from oblique angles these opposing colours will mix, creating many different colour tones. Dichroic glass is available in several different colours.

Enamels
Coloured, vitreous substances used to fire pigment into the surface of glass. These can be transparent or opaque and are normally fired at temperatures between 550°C (1,029°F) and 650°C (1,200°F).

Film
This term refers to a wide variety of vinyl products used to add safety to glass, to reduce solar gain, to reflect light, to tint glass, to reduce transparency, and to give the appearance of etched glass. Most film products are self-adhesive and are fixed to glass using water.

Firing
The process of fixing enamels into the glass in a kiln. Most vitreous enamels are fired at around 650–680°C (1,200–1,250°F).

Flashed glass
Glass with a thin layer of a different coloured glass on one side. This is produced by dipping the base glass into the second layer before blowing. *See* Antique glass.

Float glass
Sheet glass manufactured according to a patented method of floating liquid glass on top of molten tin.

Frit
A glass material that has been melted and then ground into a powder.

Fusing
Melting different layers of glass, whether coloured or clear, at around 760°C (1,400°F) so that the layers fuse into a single sheet. Some types of glass are incompatible, so special ranges of compatible glass can be purchased for fusing.

Laminated glass
Two layers of glass bonded together with an interlayer. Sometimes called "safety glass", it is resistant to breaking into pieces or shattering. The interlayer can be a poured resin or some form of "plastic" interlayer that will be cured by heat.

Low-iron glass
Glass with a higher lead content than normal float glass. This reduces the green colour of most glass and creates what is sometimes called "white glass" or, more technically, "optical glass" or "lead crystal". Low-iron glass transmits light much more effectively than regular glass, but is softer and more susceptible to scratching.

Mouth-blown glass
Glass that is blown into a "muff" (a cylinder) before being formed into a flat sheet of glass, usually roughly 600 x 900mm (24 x 35in). Also called "antique glass".

Opaque
A descriptive word often used of glass. "Translucent" would be a more accurate term, since glass usually transmits some quantity of light, whereas truly opaque materials do not.

Peppering

A process of very light sandblasting that creates a slight reduction in transparency in the glass.

Photovoltaic glass

Glass that has solar cells incorporated inside the lamination to convert solar energy into electricity.

PVB (polyvinyl butyral)

A plasticized interlayer that is heated under pressure between two layers of glass to create a laminated glass.

Resist

A material that is used to cover selected areas of glass to mask it from acid, sandblasting, or enamels.

Ribbed glass

A fairly common type of rolled, clear glass with a series of parallel ribs.

Sandblasting

A treatment whereby sand, projected by compressed air, abrades the surface of the glass.

Silverstain

A silver oxide that provides a unique method of colouring glass. During firing the stain penetrates deeply into the glass and is transparent. It then produces colours from amber to lemon yellow.

Slumping

The process of melting regular annealed glass over a mould at around 700°C (1,100°F). This is similar to the process used to bend glass, which is done at 600°C, but the extra 100°C allow the glass to sag into a finely detailed mould, creating any type of texture required.

Solar gain

The amount of heat that a structure gains through its glazed surface.

Toughened (tempered) glass

Glass that has been heated and then suddenly cooled by jets of cold air. This creates glass that is much stronger and much more flexible. When it is fractured, it will "explode" into many small fragments.

UV (ultra-violet) bonding

A technique of bonding together materials using an adhesive that is cured in ultra-violet light. These adhesives create a transparent bond that is extremely strong.

Water-jet cutting

A system of cutting shapes using high-pressure (60,000psi) water mixed with abrasives. The machines are digitally controlled and can cut virtually any shape from a piece of glass.

Mitchell Beazley would like to acknowledge and thank the following architects and artists, and photographers, for giving permission for their work to be included in this book and providing images.

Key: a above, b below, c centre, l left, r right

1 Lyle & Whitesavage/Nick Lyle; 2 José Castrillo; 4–5 Mansilla & Tunon/Roland Halbe; 6–7 Carpenter Lowings/Tim Soar; 8l & r Alexander Beleschenko/Alexander Beleschenko; 9a & b Frei Otto/Mayer/Frei Otto; 10l Patrick Heron/Andrew Moor; 10r Graham Jones/Graham Jones; 11al Udo Zembock/Udo Zembock; 11ar Fusion Glass; 11b Udo Zembock/Gerard Dorzkay; 12l Brian Clarke; 12r Graham Jones/Wilhelm Derix; 13l Engelhardt-Sellin; 13r Derix Studio; 14 Jochem Poensgen/Silke Helmerdig, Berlin; 15a StuartReid/Stuart Peto; 15b Guy Kemper/Alan Gilbert; 16–17 Dominique Perrault/Peter Kogler/André Morin; 18 Diener & Diener/Helmut Federle/Christian Richters; 19 Jean Nouvel/Philippe Ruault; 20bl, bc, br Jun Aoki & Associates/Nobuaki Nakagawa; 20al, 21a & b deLugan-Meissl/Margherita Spiluttini; 22–5 Herzog de Mueron/Margherita Spiluttini; 26–7 Herzog de Mueron/Duccio Malagamba; 28–9 Wiel Aretz/Jan Bitter; 30–3 EEA/Christian Richters; 34–39a Sauerbruch & Hutton/Jan Bitter; 39b Sauerbruch & Hutton/Jan Bitter/Markus Bredt; 40–1 Benisch & Benisch/Professor Christian Kandzia; 42, 43bl Medium Architects/Klaus Fraum; 43a & br Medium Architects; 44a & b The Buchan Group, Melbourne/Murray Hedwig; 45l Arquitectonica/John Gosling/RTKL, courtesy Arquitectonica; 45r Eduard Miralles/Rafael Vargas; 46l David Adjaye/Lyndon Douglas; 46r, 47 David Adjaye/Timothy Soar; 48–9 Will Alsop/RoderickCoyne; 50–1 Brunete Fraccaroli; 52–3 Jamie Carpenter/Andreas Keller; 54l & r Liam Gillick/Terry Farrell/Morley von Sternberg; 55 Liam Gillick/Terry Farrell/© Tim Crocker/cmpimages.com; 56–61 Hal Ingberg/Hal Ingberg; 59a Hal Ingberg/Robert Baronet [METIS 04]; 62, 63a &br ORMS/Peter Cook; 63bl ORMS/Jürgen Schmidt; 64 UN Studio; 65–7 UN Studio/Christian Richters; 68–9 Nial Mclaughlin/Nick Kane; 70–1 Nial Mclaughlin/Hufton and Crow; 72–3 Fernanda D'Agostino/Brian Foulkes; 74l Mira Maylor/Andras Suranyi; 74r Eric Hilton/Eric Hilton; 75l Graham Jones/Clay Perry; 75r Espen Tolletsen/Espen Tolletsen; 76 Odd Tandberg/Jiri Harran; 77al & ar Bridget Jones/David Lawson; 77bl Keneth Leap; 77br Sarah Hall/André Beneteau; 78a & b Martin Donlin/Paul Highnam; 79, 80b, 81 Martin Donlin/Joseph O'Callaghan; 80a Martin Donlin/Dennis Gilbert; 82, 83b Stuart & Michael/Spike Mafford; 83a Stuart & Michael; 84–5 Linda Beaumont/Spike Mafford; 86–7 Löne & Neumann/Jörn Neumann; 88–9 Amber Hiscott/David Pearl; 90–1 David Pearl/David Pearl; 92–3 Tobias Kammerer/Horst Goebel, Görsroth; 94–5 Tobias Kammerer/Martin J. Ducker, Ulm; 96–7 Sasha Ward; 98–9 Udo Zembock; 100–1 Saskia Schultz; 102–5 Brian Clarke/courtesy Ascot Racehorse and HOK Sport; 106–7 Graham Jones/Paul Highnam; 108 Graham Jones; 109 Graham Jones/Paul Highnam; 110–11 Graham Jones; 112–13 Alexander Beleschenko/Raffaella Sirtoli; 114 Alexander Beleschenko/Phillip Vile 115 Alexander Beleschenko/Alexander Beleschenko; 116–19 Stuart Reid; 120–124a Kate Maestri/Philip Vile; 124bl Yorgos Papadopoulos/Yorgos Papadopoulos; 124br Stuart Low/Clay Perry; 125 Guy Kemper/Horst Goebel; 126 Bert Glauner/Bert Glauner; 127 Bert Glauner/Alberto Moreno; 128 Peter Kuckei; 129a Peter Kuckei/The Style Republic; 129b Peter Kuckei/Glasmalerei Peters; 130 Dorothy Lenehan/Andrea Quagliata; 131 Dorothy Lenehan/Kana Tanaka; 132a Sarahko Yamamoto/Gan Tame; 132–3 Sarahko Yamamoto/Jiro Hamana; 134–5 Glass Brain; 136 Yorgos Papadopoulos; 137 Yorgos Papadopoulos/Andrew Lamb; 138–9 Chris Wood/Chris Wood; 140–1, 142al José Castrillo/Antonio I Ajusticia; 142ar & b José Castrillo; 143 José Castrillo/Anna Carlotta; 144–5, 146, 147a Tom Patti/Paul Rocheleau; 147b Tom Patti/Steve Rosenthal; 148 Fusion Glass/Philip Vile; 149al & r Mira Maylor/Yaron Leshem; 149b John Lewis/John Lewis; 150–3 Florian Lechner; 154–5 Thierry Boissel/Thierry Boissel; 156 Narcissus Quagliata/Mauricio Avramow; 157 Narcissus Quagliata/Fernando Aguilar; 158–9 Urbanowicz/Tomasz Urbanowicz; 160–161l Renato Santarossa/Horst Schmeck; 161r Renato Santarossa/Wolfram Janzer; 162 AMA/Clay Perry; 163l Shelagh Wakely/Tetsuhito Tanaka; 163ar Warren Carther/Dean Carman; 163bl Pip Tundstall/Kirsty Brooks; 163br AMA; 164, 165, 166al Warren Carthier/Gerry Kopelow; 166ar & b Warren Carthier/Henry Kalen; 167 Warren Carthier/Dean Carman; 168, 169l Markian Olnyk/Fotographica Studio; 169r Markian Olnyk/Markian Olnyk; 170–1 Andreas Horlitz; 172l Kirsty Brooks/Kirsty Brooks; 172–3 Arup Associates/Christian Richters; 173 GLB; 174 Kevin Todd/Mark Grimwald; 175 Kevin Todd; 176r, 177 Kirsty Brooks/Philip Vile; 176al & bl Kirsty Brooks/Kirsty Brooks; 178–9 Jurgen Drewer/P Bartsch; 180–1 Espen Tollefsen; 182–3 Michael Bleyenberg.